ANSWERING
—— THE ——
CALL

THOMAS SEMBER

FORWARD

This book is no way a guide to your life - after all, your life is your life - it is a summary of God's touch upon mine and I thought that after reading it you may be able to find the strength and courage in Christ in answering His call.

I am grateful if you find yourself reading this book, I thank you personally for allowing me to share parts of my life and how my God has touched me personally and has given me the opportunity to share with you for a little while. I would caution you to never replace the time you spend reading God's Word for time reading this book. For we must first and foremost spend time in the greatest love letter written to each of us, personally, from a heavenly Father who cares so much for us that He gave us the very life of His Son Jesus Christ. So please take the time to hear from God as you spend time in this book, for what I share is only one small page compared to the loving Word found in the Bible.

I would like to thank all those who have taken part in my journey here on earth and all those who have guided me and walk with me - first of course is my God, to Him be the glory - for the loving times of discipline, truth, love and the many blessings from the early years - parents that cared enough to share the love of Christ, brothers and a sister who put up with the challenges of a sibling who struggled with anger, for my wife, Carolyn, who looks past my inabilities and sees only a man trying to follow Christ, to my three daughters, Jessica, Katie and Becky, who are the joys of my union with my wife. They have been true blessings in my life.

And lastly to Steve, here it is!

ANSWERING
THE CALL

I had answered thousands of calls on the Fire Dept, but there was one call I kept avoiding. Each day of our lives, we will receive calls, some will be looking for help, others may be a call to just say hello, they may be business calls, personal calls but answering the call will always come down to the choice of whether to answer or not.

Many times, I had received a call from a friend or a stranger looking for some help, "Sure, I'm on my way!" was my reply. That was the typical answer I gave each time I heard the call but for years there was one call I kept avoiding.

The call, I kept avoiding, was a call I received when I was about 8 years old, laying on my back in the yard, looking up at the passing clouds, making believe they were this or that. Maybe you've done that too, when I heard this voice say, "If I lead, will you follow?". My first thought was that it was my dad working in the garage, so I yelled out to him, but there was no answer. I thought maybe I was hearing things, but there it was again, deep within me "If I lead, will you follow?!"

Who could be calling and why? What did they mean; if they lead, would I follow? So many questions came to mind that day. Then it hit me, being brought up in a Christian home, I thought maybe, just maybe it was God... but why would He be calling me? This was the first of many times I would hear that still small Voice deep inside but sadly never answered it or only tried to answer it the way I wanted to. Maybe you've heard that still small voice within you too; I pray that as you read, you will answer the Call.

That day in the yard was the beginning of trying to understand the question of who is calling and learning how to answer it. Throughout my life, I tried answering it in different ways but life would have twists and turns, failures and successes, before I truly understood what that Call was all about.

Like I said before, every day we get calls - whether they are on the phone, snail mail, email, twitter, snap chat, text or someone knocking at our door, someone will be calling and how we answer that call will make all the difference, that's if we choose to answer it. Sometimes the call comes when we least expect it, sometimes the call will be so loud we can't avoid it but that doesn't mean we have to answer it! Despite how and if we answer the call, the reason why we need to answer it, is more important but we'll get to that later.

As I look back now, there was one thing that kept me from answering the call. It would take me almost 30 years before I finally began to understand how to answer that call from the back yard. You see I have a problem or should I say had a problem. I first remember hearing about my problem when I was very young. I was four years old at the time, when my mom took me to see the family doctor. I don't remember that visit but she had shared it with me on more than a few occasions. My problem was that I was growing up angry. Not the typical little boy anger but an all - out rage that would take me over - yes, I said take me over - I don't remember the first few times it happened but many years later, I would understand why she took me to the doctor that day. Of course, the answer the doctor gave her that day was right but it would take years before it came to pass - his answer was rather simple, it was "he will outgrow it!"

This book is about me but then again it's not - sound crazy, well the reality is that I share my story so that you will do two things 1. Learn to listen to hear the voice of God and 2. Have the courage to Answer His Call - I would ask you, as you read this book, to pray about those two things. With each page, take some time to ask yourself those two questions and I pray, that by the time you finish, you will have learned that He is calling and find the strength to answer His Call. Like I said, this book is not so much about me as it is about God - a loving Father who cares for us and as I share His Touch upon my life, would you give Him the glory, as I do, for I am a sinner saved by His Grace. I am not a theologian, or a bible scholar, I am a man who heard a Voice say to me as a young child, "if I lead, will you follow?" and struggled through life trying to understand why God would ask me that question. Maybe He has asked you that question too! Maybe your struggling with answering it too!

Fast forward a few years from that backyard experience, I found myself answering another call. As I hung up the phone, my dad said "30th, are you sure?" I had received a call from the civil service office regarding where I placed on the entrance exam for the local Fire Dept. Up until that time, I had 23 different jobs, always leaving one job to better myself with the next, but not really having a plan for my life. The only reason I took the fire exam was to please my dad, who was on the job. He has three sons and one daughter. He kept telling us what a great job it was. Well for some reason, I was his only child who took the exam, maybe just to make him happy and yet I found myself eager to hear where I placed. "Call back!" my dad shouted, wanting to be sure I had placed 30th on the list. So I called and sure enough, 30th was what they told me. My dad had shared the fact that the fire dept. was going to have a class of 80 rookies soon, so it shouldn't be long before I joined him in the ranks of firefighter. Who would have thought that two years later, I would finally get the call to join the ranks of the Fire Dept. and follow in his footsteps! Answering that call was one of the best things I ever did, even though my career was cut short, it forced me to answer that Call that I had heard when I was just a young boy laying in the backyard, but I never would have suspected answering it would turn out the way it did.

Funny thing, back then, being newly married and having a child on the way, the call of the fire department carried stability for my family. I didn't recognize it then but am blessed to have said yes to my dad when he asked me to take the test. I wasn't really looking for the call to become a firefighter but when it came, I had a choice to answer. You will see this theme throughout these pages.. that answering the call comes down to choice. But then again, there will be those times when choice has nothing to do with the answer but everything to do with the call.

This is not a self - help book or even a theological discussion of where the calls come from. It will simply be the story of God's Call, His Call and my answer. It is meant to be an encouragement for those who can hear His Call but are not sure who is calling, why God would be calling or haven't found the courage, or the strength, to answer it.

So I guess, we can begin with, is someone calling us.. God created man; God called us to rule over the fish of the sea and the birds of the air.. I'd say that's "someone" calling us wouldn't you? Now don't get all bent out of shape, this isn't a book about how to open a fishery or a house of birds, it is simply my story of answering His Call or I should say HIStory of the Call and how answering it has lead me to where I am today.

I heard the call many times and didn't answer and the reason I used too often was, why would God be calling me, a guy with an anger problem and if He was calling (which I knew He was), how could I answer it. I'm just a man who was trying to live life and get through the struggles like most guys and don't forget, I still had this anger problem that haunted me, so why would God call an angry man to follow Him. I came to learn that God isn't looking for the perfect man to follow Him but He calls all men to follow despite our failures. You see, God doesn't see us as we see ourselves - I saw an angry guy, or maybe you see an addict, or someone who struggles with porn, a workaholic or maybe just a regular guy. God sees us as His Creation, created in His Likeness and Image. He sees us as sons of a loving Father.

Growing up, I did the usual boy things, getting into trouble, doing things that I would regret, but deep within me, I kept remembering that call from the back yard, but fought against answering it. There were times that despite that initial call, I would get this feeling as if God was asking me to do something, something others could have done but He was asking "me" to do it. You see, I kept just close enough to God to hear those calls and yet far enough away so I didn't have to answer it or wouldn't give the answer I felt He was asking for. The biggest reason I used over and over for not answering His call was the anger. It became an easy excuse to keep me from answering. The anger in my life always seemed to get the best of me right before or during a call. I told myself over and over, there's no way God could use or want me answering that call - He must have meant that call in the yard for someone else. After fighting within myself, I finally tried to answer His Call when I was 13 years old. I tried to answer it by going away to a seminary to be a Carmelite Brother, but you see that was my answer, not what He was looking for, so I came home after a year of school. I again tried to answer it my way and enrolled in a home study program to be a diocesan priest, but again, my answer, not what He was looking for, and after two years, I dropped out. Sometimes when the call comes, we try and answer it the way we think is best, only to find out that it's not how He wants us to answer. I had never stopped to ask Him what HE wanted or meant when He called me to follow Him, I kept trying to do it myself or I would choose not to answer and use my anger as an excuse.

Over the next few years, after becoming a fire fighter, I floundered about. Always having this feeling that sooner or later, I needed to answer His Call but deep within me, I always questioned why God would be calling me, for I had this anger within me. So let's talk about that anger problem. It wasn't like I walked around angry all the time. I do remember some great memories from my childhood but sadly when I think back on my life, I see a whole lot of anger, pain, tears, and hurts I have caused along the way. When you have an anger problem, you seem to relive every one of the times you lost it, or at least I do. Yes, I say "do" because even today, I can recall many times when my anger caused pain, hurting the ones I loved - one of the hardest thing I need to learn is how to let go of that pain, let go of the hurt I caused. It got so bad on some days that I even thought that life for those around me would be better if I wasn't there. Those were some pretty rough and ugly days and nights where I questioned why I was even born. I had caused so much pain, especially to those I loved, that I wasn't even sure that I wanted to face another day. It was during those darker days, when I struggled with life and why would

God be calling me to follow Him. I remember many times sitting at church on Sunday and crying out to God. I think back to the times of my anger outbursts and think how could I ever go on. The pain I caused, the words I used, and the things I did during those outbursts. I sat many nights trying to figure out where this anger came from. What was causing it? I found an easy excuse for my anger; blaming everyone else, and lied to myself that my anger was caused by what others were doing or not doing in my life. Funny how you can find blame in everyone else except yourself. Now during this time, I didn't really know I was a sinner but I knew that the way my life was going, it was going to have a happy ending, I couldn't keep hurting the people I loved. I wasn't into drugs or alcohol or any other "substance", but I let anger get the best of me, time and again. I would tell myself that I wasn't "that bad", but I felt that there was something more to this thing called life, there must be something more. If I was going to answer that call from the backyard, I had to face some truths about my life. I had been raised in a Christian Catholic home. I was an altar boy, attended the local youth group and yet…I knew that the anger I had inside had to be dealt with before I could truly answer that call from the back yard. I wasn't looking to be perfect but I didn't see how I could answer that Call without dealing with the anger first. God is not calling perfect people, He is calling us, just as we are, imperfect people. God wanted me to answer the call despite the anger, I just needed to let go of it. I really needed to grow up.

So, answering the call starts with learning the Truth about ourselves and facing somethings we might rather not face.. We may think that there's really no reason someone, especially God would be calling and yet He is. He is calling us men, not because He needs us but because He wants us. He wants us to have a relationship with Him. That relationship is available because of His Son Jesus Christ answered the call. He gave all of Himself, when God called and asked Him to go to the Cross for us. Take a moment and think that Jesus went to the Cross, all the way for us, in our sin, in my anger. Jesus gave it all for us and God will be asking that of us as well. Asking us to give all of ourselves to Him, not just the parts that we want to give. That's where I tried to answer the call, giving Him just a little part of me, not all of me. There are people calling us as well, family, wives, children and co - workers, pastors and people in our communities, calling us to answer the call of godly men in today's day, and it is time we stop finding excuses and begin to answer those calls.

Having grown up with Christian parents, being taught right

from wrong, you think I could have kept my anger in check. Not so, it was almost as if someone else or something would take over me. I guess that excuse can only work so long, like saying "the devil made me do it". The devil can't make us do anything, he only suggests, it's us who make the decision to act on it. I tried using that excuse too, the devil made me do it, when the anger got the best of me. After an anger outburst, I always tried to justify it by blaming someone else, anyone else; it was their fault I lost my cool, or the devil made me do it. I used the excuse of the fact they didn't do this or that or they did do this or that. I never looked at me… but one day I would be forced to.

I can walk into any room in my parents' house and my house today and remember the times when my anger had taken over. There are marks left on the walls of where I punched it, or threw a coffee cup and I had to wonder, what about the marks I left on the people I loved. The deep - seated marks of pain on my family, those marks don't come off or can't be fixed as easily as some walls can. Family would learn to walk on eggshells around me, making sure, what they said and how they said things to me, would not 'aggravate" me to lose my cool. The sad thing was that my anger blow - ups would never happen "in the public eye" - nope, never at work, or at school and most of all never at church. It would only happen behind closed doors, with those that I loved, with those that I was supposed to hold dearest in my life - family. There were times when my family had planned an outing of some sort and before you knew it, something would trigger me, my anger would ruin the day and we ended up not going. Then came the guilt, having brothers and sisters and having their "fun" day ruined because of my anger just made me feel worse about the whole anger problem. I remember thinking to myself that I didn't deserve any good in my life. There were times when I would strike out in anger just so other people felt as bad as I did inside. It sounds so terrible when I think back to those times, wanting others to feel bad because I was out of control. It became a vicious circle of anger, guilt, pain and then trying to find forgiveness, but I first needed to be truthful with myself, was I truly sorry for the outbursts.

As I shared before, growing up with an anger problem causes you to question why would God be calling. During those years, calls would come in …calls that I should have answered, calls I would need to answer, some I did but others I did not. Like the time I saw the kids in the neighborhood picking on one of the handicapped guys from the neighborhood…I heard the Call to step in but was too afraid to answer it…sound familiar. Or how about the time, when the guys at work decided to do a little more than just work, like taking the truck to do some "on the side work" or how about the call from a friend that he stole one of his dad's nudie books...no problem answering that call. Too often I found myself answering the wrong calls but still deep within me was the Call that I just couldn't forget, couldn't get away from, even though I had said "yes" many years ago while lying in the back yard, I kept running away from truly answering it...maybe fear, maybe I just wasn't sure how to answer it... maybe if I ignored it long enough, it would stop but deep inside I knew that part of my problem for not answering it was that my anger was more in control of my life that I was.

I had tried many different ways to hide my anger, I tried the counting to ten way of dealing with it but I never seemed to get past 2 before the full - blown anger would erupt and I once again hurt those I loved. I tried walking away, but it seemed that my anger would turn me around and I would be right back into it. I would never strike out in anger with my hands. NO I was too smart for that - it was almost as if I knew how far I could let the anger go and how far to hold it back and yet I felt it was out of my control. I know that may seem like it makes no sense but then again the anger problem made no sense to me. I felt like Paul and what he shared in Romans 7 from the Holy Bible, about doing the very thing I hate and not doing the very thing I knew was good. I knew my anger was wrong but each time the feeling would build inside of me until I lost control. As the anger grew, so did the outburst. It got to the point that I started using my hands, not on people but on things, like throwing coffee cups, punching walls, tearing things apart. The sad reality was that some of the very things I loved, I ruined. Which led to more guilt, more feeling ashamed, more hurt! There had to be a way out of the cycle I was living.

Now when most people met me, they would never have known I had this problem. Some will even be shocked when they read this, what a con artist I had become. I never talked about it to anyone but those close to me knew about it for they had experienced it firsthand. I can't say what or how they felt but let's be honest, who wants to be around someone like that! I didn't even want to be around myself, there had to be away out of it, but I wasn't sure where or how to go. I found myself not wanting to be around anyone for fear that the outburst of anger would happen and then I was left to apologize again and again. It was just easier to be alone.

There is a certain feeling of embarrassment that resides inside you, where you can't want to walk into a doctor's office and say, I'm out of control. You would rather try to hide it, until of course, it rose its ugly head again and then you went through all the emotions, feelings of being helpless, feeling so down that you weren't sure you even wanted to face another day. Knowing how bad you hurt the ones you loved and trying to apologize again and again... you even wondered if your apology was accepted and that made me feel even worse. How many times can you apologize for the same type of thing without them wondering if it was a true apology.

About the same time as the fire dept. call came in, I decided to ask a question of my own. The question was to ask a beautiful woman named Carolyn to marry me. She answered by saying yes, and so on Sept 8th 1984 we were joined as one. But even during the excitement of getting married, that old anger problem was raised. You see the night before we were to wed, my mom sat down with my soon to be wife Carolyn, and asked if her is she really knew who she was marrying. My mom wanted to be sure that Carolyn knew about my anger and temper outbursts. Although it hurt me to have my mom share that, I know she did it out of love for Carolyn and myself, wanting to spare us any pain down the road. Even with the conversation with my mom, Carolyn still agreed to marry me. What a blessing she is in my life, from saying yes to living everyday as a helpmate, friend, lover.

After getting married and getting on the fire dept., I began a second job to help make ends meet. Carolyn and I had decided that although she had her degree from college, we wanted our children brought up in a home where someone was there. A mother to love and nurture our children in the way we thought best. To be honest, the thought of having a child was scary. I didn't want our child to grow up with an angry father; that put more pressure on me to try and find out how to stop it. I thought maybe it would be best if I wasn't' around the child so I began to work. I started building houses and even started my own handyman business in the community I was living in - believe it our not, that was partly answering His Call, I just never knew it. You see, I never charged enough for the work I was doing, it was more about helping, it grew to where it became more about helping others than making money. But to be brutally honest, I worked about 150 hours a week; just to keep from being around those I loved, for fear of an angry outburst that would hurt them. I worked so hard that when it was time to come home, I was exhausted and would spend the time sleeping. It was a terrible way to live, trying to run away from the problem that seemed to keep me from answering His Call.

Throughout this entire time, God had been a part of my life, but a distant part. As a young man, I kept God at a distance, not wanting to hear that call from the backyard as a young boy…and it was every time I seemed to get closer to Him, the call would get louder, so I kept my distance. I was the man who went to church on Sundays, helped others, but yet still had the anger problem when things didn't seem to go my way. Sometimes the anger would arise because I felt that people just weren't listening to what I had to say. So I got louder, trying to make my point and if that didn't work, I would explode. I knew it was wrong and made apologies, heartfelt apologies time after time - I knew it had to stop, but couldn't or didn't know how to stop it.

For many years, the anger led my life. It's not that I walked around angry all the time but it seemed that at certain moments in my life, my anger came to the forefront and ruined the day, each outburst led to agonizing times of trying to figure out what was "wrong" with me, pleading for forgiveness for those I hurt and crying out to God for it not to happen again. I kept living just close enough to "be good" but not good enough to answer the call from my childhood. I would come to understand that I would never be good enough to answer His Call - God was calling me right where I was, in my anger, in my sin, in my struggles - God still calls - the Bible is filled with God calling men in the midst of their struggles, but I would learn that later. Maybe God is calling you right now, you can hear His Voice, but you think that your past, your addiction, your current struggles will keep you from answering, that is a lie, remember it comes down to choice! We can focus on our problems or we can focus on His Call.

Life went on this way, outbursts of anger, hurting those I loved, alienating my family and then falling on my knees praying for God to make it right, make me better, to heal the pain I was causing. Many nights I cried myself to sleep, not wanting the anger to continue. I can recall almost every time when I let the anger control me, like the time I had an outburst when my grandfather was there. I remember him telling my father, "If that was my child, I would take him out behind the shed!" so that became the pattern for my life - stay just close enough to God to know He was calling but far enough away not to have to answer and the pattern of angry outbursts would continue, then came the apology, then the guilt and the remorse for hurting those I loved.

That pattern would continue until one of my daughters found the strength to call my mom during an anger outburst in our home. My mom called the police, but we'll get to that later. Let me say here that I am grateful to God that I never laid a hand on my wife or daughters but sometimes the pain we give out by our words and actions can cause more pain than broken bones. These kinds of wounds take years if not a lifetime to heal, and sadly some may never heal. I remembered the old adage about "sticks and stones may break your bones but names will never hurt you!" sounded good but the reality is that names do hurt and hurt worse than broken bones! When I close my eyes and think, I can recall almost every time I let my anger get the best of me. When I look around my home, I can see the times and places I put my fist through the wall, or broke a coffee cup or threw an object in anger - these were constant reminders to me that I would never be able to answer the Call that I heard when I was back in my yard as a young boy. I thank God that I had never put my hands on my wife or children but the pain I did cause was inexcusable. Although my family and friends would say they forgave me, I believed the lie I heard in my head that God could never forgive me. So why did He keep calling, what was it that He wanted? I would learn that the lie, of Him not forgiving, is the farthest thing from the truth, God does forgive and not only forgives but forgets, something we humans have a hard time doing. I know today as I walk into a room with those I have hurt by my anger, that there is a certain uneasiness that is present. I had a lifetime of anger outbursts, why wouldn't they be uneasy.

I had been born into a family of loving parents, both sharing a love of God through their own way. I was raised Roman Catholic and would always remember seeing my parents praying (probably that their son would be rid of his anger) and reading God's Word, both helping out at Church, volunteering their time doing this and that - helping out where ever and when ever - and it wasn't only there. If they came across someone in need, they always tried to find a way to help - that still goes on today. I have a brother, a year older than I, a sister 4 years younger, and another brother 8 years younger, we were a loving family except for when my anger would rise up - it would always come up at the most inopportune time. Going on vacation, holidays, birthdays but please don't get the idea that it was an everyday occurrence, it would only happen sometimes, but enough times that led my family to again walk on eggshells around me all the time, or at least I felt that way. Funny thing about families, they forgive but it's hard to forget. I don't blame them for their feelings but pray that one - day, they will see, that through Jesus Christ lives can be changed. That Jesus Christ and the power of the Holy Spirit can change an angry young man. But yet, I struggled with my anger and it kept me from answering the call of that young boy in the back yard.

To me it seemed as if a week didn't go by when my anger made another memory to try and forget, more pain in a loved one's life. I have apologized more times than I care to remember...each time praying to God to take my anger away. That day, when my mom called the police, started a journey of forgiving myself and getting a handle on my anger. I had an angry outburst; a yelling that scared my children to where they huddled up in one bedroom together. My eldest daughter not sure what to do but wanting it to stop, called my mother. My mother, probably made the hardest call of her life, she called the police. When the police arrived, they put me in handcuffs and began to ask what was going on. Carolyn and I talked with them and being a firefighter, I had a connection with the police who showed up so they asked Carolyn what she wanted to do. Carolyn had agreed to let me stay in the house as long as I agreed to go to counseling. One of the worst days of my life followed two days later. The outburst had taken place on a Saturday, so early Monday morning we had a visit from a social worker to check on the children. Even though the policemen didn't take me out of the house, there was a report written and a visit from social services. I can't think about that day without tearing up for the pain still hurts. I remember sitting on the couch and watching the social workers talk to my three daughters in another room. I saw them pick up their shirts as the worker looked for bruises on them. I know that I never hit them but the bruises I caused to their heart and spirit, by my outbursts of anger, will always leave marks for their lifetime. No one should grow up with an angry father, no one! I was allowed to stay in our home and the children could stay but there would be checkups every so often for six months and if nothing else happened the case would be closed. So we began, visiting a counselor, once a week but even during those meetings, I would find myself making excuses... it was her fault, or my siblings' fault, or the guy next door, or the car driving in front of me - there were days I even blamed the weather. The key of course was that it was never MY fault, always someone else's. After 7 years of therapy, even taking enough medication to alter my brain patterns, the anger was still there, the bouts of uncontrolled rage were there...it had to stop. I would answer all the right answers in therapy but even on the ride home, the anger would arise as I yelled and screamed at my wife. I am not proud or share for any other reason than to maybe help someone else that NO ONE HAS THE RIGHT TO TREAT ANOTHER PERSON THAT WAY ESPECIALLY THE ONES WE SAY WE LOVE! So if you're in that kind of relationship, get help, you don't have to live that way, there is another way and His

Name is Jesus! He will give you the strength to say enough is enough. There are many people and organizations out there that are willing to help, don't wait another day, and find strength in Christ to make the call.

Before I was married, had a family, and been blessed with the fire department job, I answered a call that would change my life. On a Friday night, in 1979, I was invited to a prayer meeting at a local church where I heard that old familiar Voice from the back yard. Even though it was a preacher speaking, deep inside me was this Voice calling me, the same one as the one from the back yard. I remember as I sat there and heard the preacher say that God's call is open to everyone, I said to myself how could God call an angry person like me...but He was. God calls sinners and I was for sure one. This is one call I couldn't get away from. No matter how many excuses I had in my head, the preacher kept answering them. He asked for anyone that felt God calling to come forward. Finally, I came forward and accepted Jesus as my Lord and Savior. I thought, as I left the church that day, that my anger wasn't going to be a problem anymore but here I was years later still struggling with it. Remember I said I stayed close enough to hear Him but far enough away that I didn't have to answer Him.

After years of therapy, seeing different counselors, I had enough - it had to end. One Friday night, I told my wife that I was going into our bedroom to pray and not to come in no matter what she heard. What she didn't know was that I was going to cry out to God to either take the anger away or take my life. I wasn't going to kill myself but if God would not take it away, I would ask Him to take my life. I knew I had to stop living this way. So as I knelt by the side of our bed, with my bible opened, I began to pray...I began to cry out to God... take this away or take my life...I repeated it over and over until deep within me I heard that familiar voice from the back yard when I was a young boy. What I heard was "NO" ...I remember thinking to myself, hey, you are God, a God of love, take this away or take my life... this time I felt Him say "NO, it's not Mine to take" - but wait, wasn't I made in your image, in your likeness (knew just enough of God's Word to throw that in!) - Again "No, it's not Mine to take, it's yours and you must grow up, take responsibility for YOUR actions". The words from that doctor visit so long ago, repeated in my head.

No one had ever said those things to me quite that way, I remembered that time when my anger was out of control, hearing my grandfather tell my dad, "if that was my son, I'd take him out behind the shed and take care of him good", but this was different. It's not like I didn't have other moments in my life that I have heard those things, like the time I went on a rage, yelling and screaming at my dad, now my dad is 6'3", about 230 lbs....he was a marine, state trooper, an armed guard at the federal reserve bank, a lieutenant in the fire service and worked out with weights - bear claws for hands, strength to rip telephone books in half, which was the highlight of many neighbor kid gatherings...as I yelled out of controlled, screaming obscenities, spitting in his face, he grabbed me and pinned me to the floor and sat on my chest and said words that I will never forget "if it wasn't for the love of Jesus Christ, I'd knock the living crap right out of you!" And he could have done it, but it would be years later that I would learn just how much love that took. Years later, on a fishing trip, with just my dad and me, we would talk about that day in length, about how the love of Jesus kept him from taking my head off. Because of our open conversation and the love of Jesus Christ, we have a great father/son relationship today, one where we can talk about anything. Even through the anger, God was still blessing me with things like a loving father. I am in awe of God's love for us.

Now back to the bedroom as I knelt there by the side of my bed. I couldn't really believe I was hearing this from God, shouldn't He have just taken my anger away or taken my life. God was teaching me about being mature, responsible for my actions, to grow up. The call, we men need to answer each day of our lives, is to be mature, be responsible and to grow up. Easier said than done sometimes. That night, I spent time going through the Bible, it seemed like every verse I turned to spoke of anger, like "be angry but do not sin". I underlined them, read them, reread them over and over and came to realize it was time for me to grow up and be responsible for my actions. I would love to say that I had never had another anger explosion but answering the call to maturity is a growing process. Learning to grow up takes time but I can honestly say that the outbursts have stopped, if I keep answering His Call, that call from my childhood.

The journey of growing up continued when someone invited me to a men's weekend event...five of us decided to drive and attend a Christian men's weekend event. We believed what they shared at the event, about getting an accountability group started. A group of men, who met weekly to share life, share the Bible and talk Truth into each other's lives, to ask the difficult questions of life that we keep hidden deep where no one can see them. Out of that group meeting, I started my daily emails. It began as I sent daily readings from a men's resource to them at work and eventually it led to my own daily readings. They contain a scripture verse and a story of life, where I was answering the call of living out His Call. That still goes on today. You can receive them either by emailing me (tomsember@gmail.com) or going to men.ag.org and sign up to received them in your email.

But let's get back to answering the call; you know the one I kept ignoring each day. It's not that I didn't want to answer it; I just didn't have the strength, courage to answer it. You see it meant going against the grain - going against what the world deemed as "normal" - you see men don't talk about their struggles, their feelings, their sense of just not knowing how to do this thing called life. I have found in my 25 plus years of men's ministry, that all men struggle with these things and it was going to take courage to step up and answer the call - but what about the anger, what about my past and all the times I let the anger control me. I had to stop finding excuses and start answering the call.

I had to come to the realization that men struggle, even men in the Bible. Men like David who was a man after God's Own Heart. Paul who struggled with a thorn in his side, men like James and John who wanted to call down thunder to rid a problem. These and other stories about men and their struggles can be found in the greatest book ever written, it's call the Bible. Be sure to get yourself a copy and begin to read it, underline it; mediate upon it, it will change your life. But don't let it end there, get a group of men together and share your struggles, your dreams, your success and your failures. Men that will help you answer His Call of being godly men, men of His Word, men of action!

I am not sure where I first learned about answering the calls of life; maybe it was my parents who taught it to me. For 33 years, my dad answered the call on the fire dept.; my mom answered the call to neighbors, friends, and strangers when they needed help. They answered the call to help at their local church, the PTA at school, the neighborhood with someone who needed a hand, also with complete strangers, just to make them feel better and have a good day. They were great examples of how to answer the call to help. I remember sitting in restaurants and listening to my parents discuss how they were going to pay the bill of a family sitting close by. Now my parents were not overly blessed with finances but they made what they had touch people's lives. Many times I would be with my dad, as he slipped a homeless person, a little cash that he had in his pocket, or paying someone's toll on the highway, little things like that, taught me the value of answering the call. In the middle of fishing trip, we would stop and help out another fisherman who was having trouble. There were many lessons I learned from my parents about answering the calls of help.

As I look back now, I have come to realize that the call to help someone was exactly what God was asking me to do so long ago in my backyard. It was a call to share one thing, love, but most men struggle with that except when it comes to physical love - we have no problem answering that call.

So as the group of men met on Saturday mornings, to share life, God's Word and speak truth into each other's lives, I began to realize that I could answer that call it just took more of God and less of me.

Being on the fire dept. for about 19 years, I would answer a call that would change my life dramatically. It was the call where we responded to a hit and run accident where a man was injured, lying in the street. As we arrived on scene, the siren brake, on our fire engine, broke causing it to scream in the highest frequency. As the siren motor began to run out of control, the noise became deafening, so I reach and pulled out the wires running to the motor. It was a quick decision that would change my life forever. Because I was so close to the siren when I pulled the wires, the loud sound did permanent damage to my hearing. I spent the night at the firehouse trying to stop the ringing and pain in my head. I tried to hide the fact that my hearing was damaged. It wasn't until I was in another fire, in the attic with my crew, that the hearing loss would become a serious problem. The chief was calling me on the radio, to get my crew out of the attic, for fear of collapse but I couldn't hear him. One of my crew members heard the chief's call and grabbed me and we left the building. When I got outside the chief came up to me and asked why didn't I respond on the radio, my crewman simply said, Chief, he's deaf! The chief ordered me to go for a hearing test and it was found that my hearing loss was to the degree that I could no longer fight fires. I remember sitting in the Commissioners office as she said, "Tom, go clean out your locker and go home, you're done, and we will file a disability pension for you."

I couldn't believe what I was hearing or should I say reading her lips - by that time I had covered up my hearing loss by learning to read lips. As I drove from the Commissioners office to my firehouse, I remember crying and saying what will I do now - because of the disability pension, I could no longer work, no fighting fires, no house building, no handyman work...what was I going to do now...

The process of getting the disability took over two years, and during that time, I had to stay in my house Monday through Friday from 8am till 5pm in case they called me to go for drug testing - the drug policy of the department at that time. What was I going to do... funny how God has a way of working things out. About 6 months before the accident, I had begun to take some bible classes on line, to learn more about God's Word, maybe help me answer that call from my youth. As I sat home each day, I took more and more classes, more and more bible studies. At the end of two years, when I could finally leave my home during the day, I had enough course material to get certified as a minister with the Assemblies of God. I should share that after accepting Jesus as Lord and Savior, my wife and I attended an Assemblies of God church where we volunteered in different positions, she helped in girl's ministry and I, myself, with ministering to men. I found myself relating to men more and more. Talking with them about their struggles, meeting different men of different ages - the more I met with, the more I felt led to become involved in ministering to men.

I went on to be ordained with the Assemblies of God, I have held a few positions throughout the years; pastored a church, was a sectional men's leader, a regional men's leader, a state district men's director but the true answering of His Call is the men I share life with day to day. Those men, who I meet with, call, talk with, text with and share life with, is answering the call from the yard so long ago. I have spoken at many men's conferences, Royal Ranger meetings, men's bible studies, but I go where He leads, that is my answer to the question He asked years ago in the back yard. I must follow where He leads me, not bring Him along where I want to go. I answer that call as a young boy by keeping my eyes open for that man that could use a little help and the greatest help I can give them is to share Jesus Christ with them.

When God asked me if He would lead, would I follow, He wasn't asking me to lead but to follow. He wasn't asking anything but to follow Him day by day - to hear His Call daily and answer them - to truly put His Love into action. It isn't about titles, or positions, successes or failures, victories or struggles; it's simply about following where He leads. Following His Lead, answering His Call meant living by the Holy Spirit. By the power of the Holy Spirit to hear His Call and answer where He leads, brought the answer to "if I lead, will you follow"? To me, that means living Christ day - to - day, moment - by - moment. I have found a peace in my life like none other and by the way, the more I follow Him, the anger outbursts have stopped. When you put God first, and have faith in Him and let Him have control, you have nothing to fear. It was fear that kept me from answering the call from the yard, fear that people would think I was a Jesus freak, or a holy roller but I care more about what God thinks of me than anything else. By letting go of the fear, I could be the man, husband, and father He is calling us men to be. All my anger bursts were really just fear and letting go of that fear meant trusting Him in all things, and that included my life!

So I end with, if you hear God calling, and He is calling, don't be afraid to answer Him. Don't be afraid of your past, or the sins we have committed - God wants to take you as you are and make you a new man with His Strength, in His Holy Spirit power and Answer His Call!!!

Be on the alert, stand firm in the faith, act like men, be strong.
- 1 Corinthians 16:13

THINGS YOU CAN DO TO HELP YOU ANSWER HIS CALL

Pray, keep praying, and pray some more - prayer is talking to God

Accept Jesus Christ as your Lord and Savior

Get a bible, put your name in it, read it, meditate upon it

Find a good bible believing church

Get in a group of godly men, ask senior men to mentor you

Begin to build a relationship with a few men where you can be honest with your struggles

Remember that God calls us men despite our failures to be godly men, husbands, fathers, mentors, and friends!

Forgive yourself because He already has!

Now get busy answering His Call!

A DAILY CHALLENGE

A Christian Man's Resource

*Bible verses are taken from the New American Standard Bible Edition
and the English Standard Version*

2 TIMOTHY 1:8-10

[8] Therefore do not be ashamed of the testimony of our Lord
or of me His prisoner, but join with me in suffering
for the gospel according to the power of God,
[9] who has saved us and called us with a holy calling,
not according to our works, but according to His own purpose
and grace which was granted us in Christ Jesus from all eternity,
[10] but now has been revealed by the appearing of our Savior Christ
Jesus, who abolished death and brought life and immortality
to light through the gospel,

Answering the call is a daily challenge of one ordinary man's attempt at answering the call of God on a daily basis. These stories are meant to be an inspiration to answer the call God has placed in your life.

They can be used individually or in a group setting. You can read them page by page or just open the book to an individual page and start there.

Every day we will get calls... whether they come via the phone, texts, Facebook, Snapchat, Twitter, Instagram or possibly a knock on our door, they will come! If and when we answer will come down to choice, but there are those calls that come, that will have nothing to do with our answer but everything to do with who is calling... those we must answer!

This book is a collection of devotions to help in Answering the Call. Life can become so busy that we let calls go unanswered. Some calls we need to answer.

It is meant to be an encouragement to Answer the Call God is asking of us each day!

Peace,
Tom

MATTHEW 5:16

Let your light shine before men in such a way
that they may see your good works,
and glorify your Father who is in heaven.

Let me see…if I counted them all up there would be 25 in all…I pray that I have found my last one but I don't think I have. I am referring to the number of jobs I have had in my life up to this point…I started out helping dad with the family business and then cut grass at the school I was attending, went to work for a florist for awhile, even spent the day as a plumbers assistant…I have never been fired and always quit to move on to something that either paid better or seemed to fit me better. I look back on them now and realize that each job taught me different things about life… the florist - to enjoy the beauty of a rose, the plumber's assistant - didn't want to dig ditches all day long, even with the fire dept - learned the value of human life and as a director for Men's Ministry - I have learned just how much men are hurting and seem generally lost in what God is calling them to do - we sometimes settle for an occupation because it pays the bills but deep inside we are miserable about going to work…I would never tell anyone to quit their job but I believe that when you find that place that God is calling you to - where it's more than a job or occupation - you find a certain peace about going day after day - although Men's Ministry is exhausting with travel, phone calls, speaking engagements and so much more - I find at the end of the day - I have a joy and peace about what I am doing…so if you find yourself in a place where you're not sure if this is where you should be…why not take the test drive on another occupation that might not bring as much cash into your pocket but the peace in your heart is more pay than you will ever need… where is HE calling you to be…

Peace,
Tom

ROMANS 12:2

"And do not be conformed to this world,
but be transformed by the renewing of your mind,
so that you may prove what the will of God is,
that which is good and acceptable and perfect."

We are the only ones who really know what we are about .. what I mean is, when we are alone - when no one else is around - that's when we find out if we truly know and live Jesus Christ. I am not a world traveler by any sense of the word - hey I 'm not even an out state kind of guy - my life can usually be found in about a 100 square mile radius so when I do get the opportunity to travel outside my immediate life circle - it's out there when I get to find out who I really am - am I the same servant of Christ when no one knows me - do I hold tight to His Ways or am I the kind of guy who just talks the talk and walks the walk when it's easy - to be in an airport in some other city and sit down to read His Word - do I? Am I ashamed to pull out my Bible in public or is it just for Sunday morning service. If I see someone needing help - do I jump up and offer it or can I hide behind the multitude of people because no one knows me .. if I have been transformed deep inside, the answer to those types of questions is obvious but if I have not buried His Word deep within me, and learned what it really means to be a follower of Christ then the answer is that I don't really know what it means to live Jesus - walking with Christ is a day to day thing - yeah, when we accept Him as our Lord and Savior we are saved from the powers of hell and death but if He lives IN us - we must live Him OUT there, so are we? ..

Peace,
Tom

PSALM 127:2

It is vain for you to rise up early,
To retire late,
To eat the bread of painful labors;
For He gives to His beloved even in his sleep.

I had been working about 120 hours a week, going from one job to another and I thought I was giving love to my family. I have been down this road - where it was all about work and the money - funny thing - the people that matter most to me (my wife and children) who I thought I was loving, were actually the ones who were being hurt - thinking somehow that the more money I made, the more I was loving them. I didn't love them; I was hurting them by taking myself out of the picture. Think about it, what would you rather have... a hundred dollars or a person who cares and loves you - the sad reality is some of us say the hundred - that's choice - I pray that we all choose to follow God's rhythm for our lives and not try to make it about the work but about the love. If we take one thing from today's verse, let it be that we need to take time out of working like a dog to re-examining our priorities, and learn that love is being there!

Peace,
Tom

PHILIPPIANS 3:10-11

[10] that I may know Him and the power of His
resurrection and the fellowship of His sufferings,
being conformed to His death;
[11] in order that I may attain to the resurrection from the dead.

Every morning I wake up and put my hearing aids in and I have to admit there are days when I just don't want to put them in. I wonder to myself "why God? Why" and then I take time to think about how my life has changed since getting the hearing aids - how through the deafness, that I was able to hear the Lord calling, I think about the lives He has touched through my deafness, and I think - I would go through it all again - you see when it becomes about me - then I have lost my focus - Jesus and the Fathers Will, plan and purpose - each of us have struggles - each of us have one thing or another that we are struggling with today - spend some time in prayer and to come to a place where we understand that the pain and suffering we go through makes us stronger - if we go through trials and don't learn then we inevitably go through them again and again - I don't know about you but once is enough for me - Praise Him through the struggles for He is building character in us of Christ

Peace,
Tom

PSALM 27:13-14

[13] I would have despaired unless I had believed
that I would see the goodness of the Lord
In the land of the living.
[14] Wait for the Lord;
Be strong and let your heart take courage;
Yes, wait for the Lord.

I never felt the pain of the waiting but I see it in their eyes.. as a young boy, I was blessed with an athletic ability, so when the teams began to pick sides, I usually went in the first group but there stood the ones wanting to play but seemed to always get picked last.. it may not seem like a big deal as to where you are picked but as a young boy, it told you just where you stood in the group.. after a few times of watching the faces of those picked last, I made a promise to myself that if I was ever named captain, I would make my picks a little different.. the despair in waiting can be overwhelming, so we take comfort from today's scripture as we wait.. for an unanswered prayer, a phone call from a loved one, a misdeed to be forgiven.. we find courage as we wait, in the Lord..

Peace,
Tom

PHILIPPIANS 4

The things you have learned and received
and heard and seen in me, practice these things,
and the God of peace will be with you.

I thought about mentoring - I thought to myself "who can I get to know, who can give me some good advice, have words of wisdom, who can I partner with" - and then it hit me - I was thinking a lot of what that person would do for me and my life - well the word partner to me was completely lost - it became about me - what about me mentoring someone else - what did I bring to the table (sort of speak) - I needed to take a good look at my life and was there anything that I could offer to someone else and I thought - every one of us have learned things through our life - through the ups and downs we have lived and I bet that each of us have some great advice to share - Paul tells us to keep putting into practice what we learned from him and God of peace will be with us - (today's bible verse) - loving one another is the best thing we can "practice" - pray that God sends someone into our lives that we can partner up with to mentor to each other - "in giving we receive" -

Peace,
Tom

PROVERBS 23:15-16

*15 My son, if your heart is wise,
My own heart also will be glad;
16 And my inmost being will rejoice
When your lips speak what is right.*

My wife and I have sat in the audience of many awards ceremonies for our daughters, each time we walk away a little prouder of them and give God the glory for the wisdom they are learning. Living is to become wise, that's if we really want to live…We must remember that being a parent or mentor to someone is not changing them into what we want or think they should be - it's about giving godly advice to encourage them to be the godly person that He has called them to be. We must remember that there is a responsibility to live godly lives ourselves - we can't just tell someone the words - we need to live it - and when we receive some godly wisdom from another, we need to have our hearts open to the Truth. We need to be examples, witnesses of Christ in our world, and share that with others- don't let fear keep us from being godly parents/mentors - trust in the Lord and seek His Will.

Peace,
Tom

PSALM 37:30-31

*30 The mouth of the righteous utters wisdom,
And his tongue speaks justice.
31 The law of his God is in his heart;
His steps do not slip.*

With two lug nuts broken, we knew we needed to find out what we were doing wrong. We called our dad at the firehouse and told him what had happened - very simply, without judging us, he told us to look at the stud and see if there was an "L" stamped on it - there was and he said - "guys that stands for left handed thread" - we were turning the nuts the wrong way - the rest came off no problem- our dad gave the advice without judging us - we had to swallow our pride to accept his advice and call for help - don't be afraid to admit we need help - especially from God himself and those of godly council. Men of godly council will be men who follow today's verse... is God calling us to be men of godly council...

Peace,
Tom

1 TIMOTHY 4

Take pains with these things;
be absorbed in them,
so that your progress will be evident to all.

Hey - have we ever seen someone or had to deal with someone who gave the least amount of energy possible to a project? Could we see it on their face that they wanted to be anywhere but here? Have we ourselves been in the same boat - you know only giving a part of ourselves to the task at hand - When I was first married - I was only giving part of myself to my wife - I wanted to be in the relationship when things were good but I had forgotten about the marriage vow that says "good times AND BAD". I was only giving myself during the good times, the laughs, the joys but when it came time for the pain and the tears - I was emotional and sometimes physically gone - and that just isn't right according to God's design - as I began to understand this truth, I began to look at other areas in my life - was I only giving 50% in those areas too?? I began to try and give 100% in everything - that meant that I need to see fixing the kitchen sink as a time when I need to give all of me - to do the best job I was able to do - when we mentor or are mentored we need to give the same 100% in giving of ourselves and 100% in receiving what has been shared with us - yes even the criticism - that's the hard part - - but with the Holy Spirit with us we can handle the truth! So how much of yourself are you giving... 50%, 75% - how about giving 100%, you'll see the difference!!

Peace,
Tom

ROMANS 5:8

But God demonstrates His own love toward us,
in that while we were yet sinners,
Christ died for us.

I don't like to think about it long for it scares me deep down to my core but what if...there was no God. For me personally, I do not think I would be where I am today. I think that my life would have taken a far different course, you see growing up, I was a child who was, more times than not, driven by anger. It wasn't that I was bad all the time but the things I have done in my rage...well let's just say I am not proud of them and although I know I have been forgiven and even started to forgive myself, if it wasn't for the love of my parents, family, my wife and many who I have hurt along the way - I would never come to understand who God is to me. A loving and forgiving God, who cared so much for me and wanted me to know His Love that He gave the life of His Son - and not just gave His Life but a life given to pain and suffering and death on a Cross to show me just how much He loves me...so for me God is a forgiving love - who is God to you .

Peace,
Tom

1 PETER 2

"you also, as living stones,
are being built up as a spiritual house for a holy priesthood,
to offer up spiritual sacrifices acceptable
to God through Jesus Christ."

There is no perfect church (well besides the body of believers in Christ - an even now we are not perfect but when He comes again we shall be like Him perfect in every way!) Many have said and I would agree - the church we attend has to do with the religion we belong to - knowing Christ is a relationship - which is more important? The relationship with Christ, of course! Well then, why go to church - because we are called to be part of the body of Christ - we should go to exercise that gift given to us - can you imagine the impact on society if everyone first went to church and second those that attend went so to serve others - wow can you imagine where the church families would be - there would be such an awakening by the unbelieving world to want to know more about Christ - in every church there will be conflict, disagreement and even hurt feelings but how we handle them is the real relationship we have with one another - that is where we need to be more Christ like - so why are you going to church - maybe we should be going to God first...

Peace,
Tom

AMOS 5:23

"Take away from Me the noise of your songs;
I will not even listen to the sound of your harps.

Hello - today's bible reading may seem a little harsh at first - why would God say that He would not listen to our praise? I believe the answer is found earlier in the chapter where God says "Seek Me that you may live" - if we live for any other purpose than He Himself, we are living to an end that is death - We are to put God first above all else - that means that we allow God to rule in our lives. God rules only if we acknowledge Him and His Ways - we can lie to ourselves and others that God matters, if we continue to seek the pleasures of our own self - we lie to Him and He does not want to be second in our life but first - the first in EVERTHING - will we make God first in our lives? Will we put ourselves into His Hand and say use me, mold me - SEEK HIM THAT WE MAY LIVE
Peace,
Tom

ROMANS 5:

But God demonstrates His own love toward us,
in that while we were yet sinners,
Christ died for us.

Every day I thank God...I guess you could say that there is much to be thankful for but I always thank God for one thing in particular…it is for my wife. Despite learning that I had anger problem, and experiencing it in our marriage, she still chose to love me. In being part of men's ministry, I have heard many stories of where a wife has chosen to leave the relationship when things got hard, but not my wife. She has stayed by my side and has comforted me, told me I was wrong, shared with me her intimate feelings and shared the love of God with me and for that I am grateful. That is what I thank God for each day because I know she came from Him…I have rediscovered and each new day discovered the huge heart of God. To discover God, maybe we need to slow down and take a good long look at our lives and discover just how much He loves us, because the reality is none of us are worthy to receive anything especially the life of His Son…and yet He does love us and sent His Son for us! What are you thankful for?

Peace,
Tom

JOHN 19:30

Therefore when Jesus had received the sour wine,
He said, "It is finished!" And He bowed His head
and gave up His spirit.

I hope we take some time to meditate on what occurred so many years ago - I wonder if the apostles could tell by Jesus' words to them or His Actions that things were going to change - Jesus was coming to the close of His Life on earth - He was about to finish the job the Father had asked Him to do (for us) - He was making the one and only payment for our sins - paying it in full - - - so often we go only part way - the job is left partly done or slightly unfinished - we use excuses like: we'll get to it later, that's good enough, not to worry, no one will notice - I thank God, Jesus didn't have our same excuses when it came to paying our debt - He went all the way - "it is finished!" May we remember those words and start a new beginning in Him to finish what He has asked us to do - I had some work done on my car at my uncle's auto shop, I didn't have enough to pay the whole bill so I gave him what I had. I went back the next day to pay the rest what I owed - but he said what bill - we agreed on a price the other day and that was final - there was no debt to pay - as far as he was concerned my debt was paid in full and there was nothing I could do about it - Our debt was paid in full by Jesus Christ and there is nothing we can do about it but accept it and praise his Name - what a Savior we have in Jesus; did you know that your debts been paid?

Peace,
Tom

HEBREWS 12:10

For they disciplined us for a short time as seemed best to them,
but He disciplines us for our good,
so that we may share His holiness.

       I pray today's reading finds us examining our relationships - those with our parents and those with our children but also our relationship with our Heavenly Father - for years, I was not the father I wanted to be - I knew all the right things to do but found them out of reach - I would yell - loud - I thank God that He kept me from ever laying a hand on my children in my fits of anger but the yelling was worse - I believe that it takes longer to heal that kind of hurt, but I thank God He showed me the Light - I'm thankful for my wife, for having the strength to take a stand and my mom for loving me enough to take the hurt in helping me. Today I live for Jesus and in that living I find myself really loving my children and that means times when discipline has to happen, it is done with love - to teach them God's ways so they too can love .. and to think that God gives second chances - thank God or else I would be out of the game .. how about you .. have you been the best son or daughter or the best mom or dad - or how about the best child of the living God?

Peace,
Tom

COLOSSIANS 3:13

bearing with one another,
and forgiving each other,
whoever has a complaint against anyone;
just as the Lord forgave you, so also should you.

Most of you know about my life and the battle I had with anger - what most of you don't know is that I had been blessed with a wife who stood by me through it all and even when I was at my worst she continued to love me - each time that I would come back and say those words "I am sorry" she would forgive me and we would start fresh - I think of the pain that she took for me and that's when I realized that she showed me the love that Jesus showed each of us as He was on the Cross and said those words "Father forgive them for they know not what they do". We must learn how to forgive as Christ forgave us - we must be willing to learn how to forgive as well as to be able to be forgiven - we all have faults - we all sin and fall short - and through the precious blood of Jesus we are forgiven - but the first part is repentance - a turning away from that sin and a turning to God - do we need to seek repentance in our relationship with each other -

Peace,
Tom

JOHN 17:2

I in them and You in Me,
that they may be perfected in unity,
so that the world may know that You sent Me,
and loved them, even as You have loved Me.

There were 14 of us who had decided to go and help our brothers out in NYC after the planes hit on 9 - 11, the only problem was that the powers to be did want us to go and tried to stop us...as we met in the fire house, we discussed what we should do. Like myself, many of us felt an urge, a calling to go and help in any way we could - sure there were legal options to think about, what would happen if we got hurt or killed, but the desire in each of our hearts was to help, so we joined together and made a decision that we had unstoppable unity in regards to going to Ground Zero, to help our fellow fire fighters and others who we suffering. So we boarded a train late Tuesday night and traveled all night to get to there by morning; the day after the planes hit. One of the things I remember most of the journey was the family members of those who were returning to NYC from being away - they were scheduled to return on that train without ever knowing that the planes would hit. As we sat there and people began to find out who we were and where we were going, they began to bring us pictures of their loved ones and ask us to help find them…they began to pray with us and for us - for God's touch upon the work that we were heading to…they began, in the middle of their own suffering, to pray for our safety…joining forces to follow where He leads can have unstoppable unity IF we focus on HIM and what HE is calling us to do…where is He calling us today…will we join others in that call? -

Peace,
Tom

ROMANS 10:14

How then will they call on Him in whom they have not believed?
How will they believe in Him whom they have not heard?
And how will they hear without a preacher?

Who would have thought that walking a dog would allow you to share the message of the Gospel? Each morning as I walk our family dog, I get a chance to meet some of my neighbors that are up early and going to work. They have become accustom to me and Dee walking by and saying a friendly hello as they get in their cars to drive to work. Each morning we take the same route and in doing so we get to meet the neighbors…the ones leaving for work, the lady who delivers the morning paper, the other dog owners out walking, even the early morning joggers and walkers…and I have noticed that as each day passes, the friendly hellos turn into "hey how are you doing" or "beautiful day, isn't it" and then some days the conversation goes a little longer to where we exchange names and even talk a little more. Some even will answer that things have been going a little tough for them and it is then that I can say that I will pray for them…who would have thought that walking a dog could open doors for sharing Christ… so what do you say - let's not wait for them, let's start saying hello to our neighbors…

Peace,
Tom

COLOSSIANS 4:8

For I have sent him to you for this very purpose,
that you may know about our circumstances
and that he may encourage your hearts;

My job was to carry the hose, the pump operator was to deliver the water, other men had other jobs - not everyone was called to do the same job. Each firefighter who arrives on scene has a specific job to do and the chief has the responsibility to encourage us to do our job well. I pray that today's verse will help open our eyes to being an encouraging person - now not all of us will be that and if it doesn't seem like that's the gift given to you - it's okay - let me say that again IT'S OK - we are all the Body of Christ and we all can't be hands - some of us have to be feet, or mouth pieces or hearts, or prayer warriors - so if we are saying I am not good at this - IT"S OK! God has blessed you with another gift - the key is to keep searching - and trying, and using the gift He gave to bring Glory to Him - all of you who are reading this are an encouragement to me - that you take the time and read these messages - and then some of you want to pass them on - thank you for that - May His Spirit continue to walk with each of us unfolding new truths every day and to God be the glory -

Peace,
Tom

COLOSSIANS 3:17

Whatever you do in word or deed,
do all in the name of the Lord Jesus,
giving thanks through Him to God the Father.

I am always amazed how we refer to people by their occupation - oh he's a plumber or he's a banker or she's a homemaker. Wouldn't it be nice to refer to each other by something other than what we do? And wouldn't it be great if people could tell we were Christians without us saying a word - no not by the shirts we wear or the bracelet that says WWJD (what would Jesus Do) but by our actions as Christians - there is that old time song - they'll know we are Christians by our love by our love.. Can they see us living Christ all the time or do we do it when it's convenient? Are we really part of God's team - - fighting for His Will to be done or is it about us and what we can get out of life.. some tough questions we need to ask ourselves.. if someone were to meet us for the first time, would they know we are Christians by our love.. by our love for others not ourselves..

Peace,
Tom

JOHN 3:27

John answered and said,
"A man can receive nothing
unless it has been given him from heaven.

Ever thought about belonging to God's family business - we, who call ourselves Christians, are in the "family" business - so often we think that all we have is because of who we are or what we have done but the reality is all we have is from Him - I, myself, can get caught up in Satan's lies that I have what I have because of what I have done - baloney! - All I have is from God and getting to that point can be tough but not impossible - we fall to the daily pressures of thinking we are in charge when in reality we work for a great Boss if we would recognize HIM and stand up for Him. We were created for one reason - to bring glory to God - how we do that is up to us - but we must realize the example we are sharing with the rest of the world when we say we are Christians and then beat each other up trying to race to be first or to be called the greatest, or making it all about ourselves - let's make it all about HIM today.. .

Peace,
Tom

JOHN 13:7

Jesus answered and said to him,
"What I do you do not realize now,
but you will understand hereafter."

Whether we are accountants or doctors or lawyers or housewives or congressman or struggling on welfare - we should be about our Father's business - doing the Lord's work is not just helping out at church - it's the day to day stuff - you know loving each other - serving each other - getting off our high horses and really serving - Jesus set such a great example and yet we find within ourselves reasons not to humble ourselves in service of the Lord to each other. Can you imagine what the body of Christ (us believers) could accomplish for HIM if we really all engaged into the family business - can you imagine how it would be - - when someone stumbled - another would be there to comfort and lift up.. that it was more about helping out our neighbor than ourselves. The verse before today's bible verse is where Jesus washed the feet of His disciples - in view of the pain and suffering He was going to go through at the Cross - He didn't whine about it or make excuses or need a vacation or come up with any excuse - He led by humble servant leadership - I ask us all today - are we serving God by serving each other ... .

Peace,
Tom

PSALM 81:6

"I relieved his shoulder of the burden,
His hands were freed from the basket.

When I ran around trying to fit everything in a day - I would often miss the most important time of the day - time spent in His Presence - time spent in His Word - I am getting better but still have a ways to go - I like to spend time with my dad, my earthly father, we both enjoy fishing and many times we have agreed to one day a week of fishing - but when he calls to see what day we are going - I have the all too familiar "I have too much to do this week - maybe next week". The song "Cat's and the Cradle" comes to mind where the singer talks about his life and the growing up of his son - spending time with him and then when the son is grown he is just like his father - not able to spend time together because of the pressures of life - the father finally realizes that his son has grown up just him - no time for anything but the problem and pressures of the day - - - when was the last time we took the day and spent it with loved ones, just being silly or enjoying a quiet time - when was the last time we spent more than a few minutes in prayer asking God for this and that and really sought His Face just to praise Him - our time, on this earth, is a gift from God - how are we spending it?

Peace,
Tom

ISAIAH 64:4

For from days of old they have not heard or perceived by ear,
Nor has the eye seen a God besides You,
Who acts in behalf of the one who waits for Him.

I don't like to wait in line at the store, or wait in the waiting room for a doctor's appointment. Maybe you don't either. Sometimes we view our time waiting as "wasted time", but in waiting for the things of God, there is a lesson for us - possibly patience, possibly in waiting we learn new things along the way - the reading for today could talk of Abraham and Sarah and their waiting on the Lord for the son that was promised - but they could not wait and Abraham slept with Hagar - another story - you see Sarah tried to "rush" the Hand of God - do we find ourselves "rushing" God - trying to force His Hand or worse - trying to change His Mind to what we want.. waiting can be a time of learning or it can be "wasted time" - it all depends on our motive .. have a blessed day -

Peace,
Tom

HEBREWS 4:12

For the word of God is living and active
and sharper than any two-edged sword,
and piercing as far as the division of soul and spirit,
of both joints and marrow,
and able to judge the thoughts and intentions of the heart.

I was in a book store the other day and began to look at all the self - help books - there are hundreds - and people were looking at them and purchasing them - things like "how to be a better lover" How to be a better employee" "how to lose weight" "how to succeed in life" etc. - but when you go to the religious aisle and look at the bibles - there aren't too many people there - - - if we were going on a journey or a trip - - don't we read the maps and the pamphlets that are available to make sure we don't go the wrong way or miss the important things .. this life is a journey - a place of growing to maturity - and we all will leave here someday and go on to eternity so why wouldn't we read the Best Instructions Before Leaving Earth (get it BIBLE)(thanks Carl) - I pray that we take some time and open God's Word .. to read the best book available to us about life..

Peace,
Tom

HABAKKUK 2:2

Then the LORD answered me and said,
"Record the vision And inscribe it on tablets,
That the one who reads it may run.

How many of us have heard people say that the Bible is too tough to read especially the old testament.. how many of us have even said it .. but how many of us have taken the time to really try to read the bible.. as I laid in bed last night, I read the introduction of proverbs in one of the many bibles that I have.. it stated how the book of proverbs was sayings and statements of wisdom that covered every aspect of human life - from business dealings to personal relationships to marriage etc. - and when we take the time to read it, we can agree but we need to take the time - giving God an opportunity to allow our minds to open up to the Spirit of the Word. I am always fascinated at the fact that the Bible is so personal - you can read one verse and I can read the same verse and the Spirit will speak to each of us for what He has for us - wow - - - I pray that we take an honest moment and give God's Word a chance but again it's choice - I can sit on the couch and watch TV or I can turn it off and read a verse or two.. choice - what will we choose today..

Peace,
Tom

LUKE 10:26

He said to him,
"What is written in the Law?
How do you read it?"

Reading God's Word and accepting it on His Terms - the question is, do we even open the Bible - do we even own one - I remember the first time I highlighted my Bible - a truth of God's Word jumped off the page - so many of us and our children and our friends don't take the time to read His Word - we spend countless hours reading other things like newspapers and sports books and novels - love stories and adventure stories and suspense stories - well guess what - the Bible has all that and more - but don't read it for all that stuff - read it for what it is .. THE VERY WORD OF GOD.. or are we afraid of what He might say to us and how we are living ..

Peace,
Tom

REVELATION 10:8-9

The voice from heaven called ...
"Take the unrolled scroll from the angel ... and eat it"

I wonder - if most people don't read the bible because they just don't believe that it's real - like could there really be a man who spent time in the belly of a big fish or about a group of people trying to build a temple to God or about two brothers fighting over their offering to God, or walls of a city coming down because of a shout and a trumpet blast, or about a boy who faced a giant, or an old man and woman having a child and then being willing to offer that child to God, or a farmer who plants his seed, or a man who walks on water, who heals the sick , gives comfort to the down trodden, gives sight to the blind, raises men from the dead, shares His own body and blood, and a Man who loves us so much that He was willing to die just for YOU .. we should read the bible because it's God's Word to us about life .. why not give it a try - you may just like it - oh yeah I learned last night that there are over 30,000 promises from God in the Bible - how many do you know?.. .

Peace,
Tom

EZRA 7:10

*Ezra had determined to study and obey the law
of the Lord and to teach it to the people of Israel*

Recently I had a young man say that he doesn't get anything out of hearing God's Word. I reminded him that what we get out of things depends on what we put into them, that will determine what we get out of it. If we read the Bible to have a relationship with Jesus Christ for our own gain - then it's the wrong reason - if we look at the Holy Word of God for what it really is and show the respect and fear that is due - our eyes will be open to the Truth and to revelations that we never dream possible - but it takes us to OPEN, the BIBLE - with a heart ready to hear God's Word - His very Voice to us - are you ready to hear from God??? Then grab our bibles and spend some time with God.. and remember, it's what you put into it, to get the most out of it... how much are you putting in...

Peace,
Tom

MATTHEW 7:24

*"Therefore everyone who hears these words of Mine
and acts on them, may be compared
to a wise man who built his house on the rock.*

Even before we placed the steel beams in, there was work to be done.. we had started another house build but before we put the steel beams in place, we needed to make sure that the foundation was plumb and level or else all our building would have been off.. people don't realize that if a foundation is off by a half an inch, by the time your reach the second floor, your walls, ceilings, windows, doors will be off about a good two inches.. I loved building houses, getting the walls up, placing plywood on the roof but I knew that if the foundation was off, there was going to be trouble.. today's scripture shares about houses being built upon the rock.. we need to build our spiritual house upon the Rock of our Salvation, Jesus Christ.. maybe that's what so many "houses" are a little off these days.. just saying'

Peace,
Tom

PSALM 40

How blessed is the man who has made the Lord his trust,
And has not turned to the proud,
nor to those who lapse into falsehood.

Sometimes we can get so caught up in the pursuit of happiness that we miss the blessings along the way…when I was working about 120 hours a week, I thought I was giving my best to my family. Trying to make sure we had enough finances to cover any material thing they needed or wanted. It wasn't until the accident when I received a little card that simple said - "you don't have to be a fire fighter to be our hero" did I begin to understand that work and what it produced was not the gift my family needed. They needed their dad! With God supplying our finances today, I find that I have more time for the little blessings along the way, like a quiet walk with one of my daughters, or the hug in the middle of the day, gazing at the stars with my wife, watching the evening sunset, or simple time spent laughing at some funny jokes we share. Those "gifts" are from God and are worth so much more than any store - bought gift I could ever give…sometimes the best things in life are FREE - satisfying our craving for happiness is finding out that happiness is all around us, if we take the time to see the blessings…may we take some time today and look with our spirit to see the blessings He has for us today.

Peace,
Tom

PHILIPPIANS 4:9

The things you have learned and received
and heard and seen in me, practice these things,
and the God of peace will be with you.

As we sat around the table, my wife, three daughters, son - in - law, and the two young men dating my other two daughters, it occurred to me that I was passing on something I learned from my father. It was dinnertime and we had all come together to share a meal and before we ate, before anyone took a bite, we bowed our heads to give thanks to God and ask His Blessing upon our meal. We have done this whether we are sitting in our home or out in a restaurant Anytime family gets together is a special day and my dad was on my mind, I realized that I was passing on the tradition, the practice of saying a blessing before we ate because of the example my dad had taught me. It was what I saw him do time and again no matter where we sat to eat, at home, in a restaurant or even grabbing lunch in the boat. I continue because of his example, his lesson to his children to give thanks and as the scripture for today states, there was a peace among us. What example are we teaching, by how we live, something to think about, as those younger eyes are watching and learning!

Peace,
Tom

MATTHEW 11:28-30

[28] *"Come to Me, all who are weary and heavy - laden,*
and I will give you rest.
[29] *Take My yoke upon you and learn from Me, for I am gentle*
and humble in heart, and you will find rest for your souls.
[30] *For My yoke is easy and My burden is light."*

We don't like to talk about it but we must, in order to understand what happens to our joy...there is a spiritual force that wants nothing to do but rob us of our inner joy and peace that God so desperately wants us to enjoy with Him. That force is called by many names; Satan, the devil, evil...the list could go on and on. The Word says that he even disguises himself as an "angel of light". I know myself that even being busy, thinking I am doing the right thing or God honoring can be part of Satan's plan to rob me of my joy. Someone once sent me an email that said BUSY is "Being Under Satan's Yoke" - I thought that was pretty good, for there are times we can become so caught up in this and that, where we think we are busy doing the Lord's work when in fact we are so busy that we miss the opportunities for joy... you see the devil is a killjoy and wants nothing else but to kill our joy...the question is - "WILL WE LET HIM STEAL OUR JOY OF THE LORD?"

Peace,
Tom

ISAIAH 40:26

*Lift up your eyes on high
And see who has created these stars,
The One who leads forth their host by number,
He calls them all by name;
Because of the greatness of His might
and the strength of His power,
Not one of them is missing.*

I wonder if we have ever taken the time to really look at the universe around us. It's not just looking at our planet earth; it is looking at His universe in all HIS glory. Today's reading deals with the stars in the evening sky .. I am always amazed that even though we do not see them during the daylight hours - they are still out there - still shining brightly as if on a dark night where we can see them all - I don't do it as often as I would like but to sit with my wife on a starlit night is truly fascinating - she has studied them and can point out different constellations in the sky - I love to hear her say - look over there that's .. and over there is .. it truly is fascinating but only if we take the time to look - so often in the busyness of our day, we allow the many wonders of God's creation to simple pass without ever taking the time to look .. I wonder what blessings we may be looking past as we go about our daily routines so engrossed with our day that we miss HIS Day! - Take some time to really look at the wonders around and maybe say a "thank you" to our God!

Peace,
Tom

PHILIPPIANS 1:28

*in no way alarmed by your opponents -
which is a sign of destruction for them,
but of salvation for you, and that too, from God.*

Our walk with Christ will not win any popularity contests, in fact we may just loose some of our friends along the way - today's verse speaks of being alarmed by our opponents, those who fight against us and speaks of salvation for you from God. These are values we need to keep in mind, but we first have to assume that our values are the ones that match up with God's Word - that we are in fact living the values that we are about to share and that takes a good self - examination as to what we stand for - you know the old saying "people in glass houses.." Before we get started let's re - examine what we stand for .. is it the Truth that we hold dear to our hearts.. is it more about Him than ourselves .. in the quiet moments of our life, when no one is around to check up on us, are we standing firm upon the Rock of our salvation .. or do we hold the old line of "do as I say not as I do" as the benchmark for our living .. I know tough questions for a morning but then again nowhere in the Word does it say that following Christ will be an easy road.. it wasn't for Him as He carried the Cross for us .. what are we carrying for Him..

Peace,
Tom

PROVERBS 17:22

A joyful heart is good medicine,
but a broken spirit dries up the bones.

After attending the day at a funeral for a dear old friend, and having meetings the rest of the day, I was exhausted - the last thing I want to do was anything involving muscle movement - I really wanted to just sit back and grab a book or watch a movie but our dog Dee was cooped up all day in her crate and as a border collie lab mix of only 3 years old, she had endless energy…so off to the back yard we went. She is a Frisbee nut - leaping about 6 feet in the air to grab it as I throw it to her - well, as we started out, I have to say that I was less than enthused about the whole thing but you know what…as the minutes ticked by I found myself enjoying it - each time I threw it she seemed to jump higher and higher and by the end of the night I was running around like a five - year - old, rolling around in the yard as the snow came down and Dee rolling right along with me. It ended up being just what I needed to shake off the day! Today's scripture shares about a joyful heart being good medicine but a broken spirit dries up the bones - enjoying life can start out as not what we had in mind but if we embrace the pleasure, we may just find ourselves enjoying life… even rolling around in the snow like a kid again! Take a moment to enjoy God's blessings and find the joy of the Lord

Peace,
Tom

PSALM 71:18

"And even when I am old and gray,
O God, do not forsake me,
until I declare Your strength to this generation,
your power to all who are to come."

Watch your fingers, this machine bites! I trained at my new job on the press at a local magazine printing company, the grey haired man walked me through each step of the job, when we came to the cutter, he held up his hands, missing one finger on one hand and two on the other! That is when he said watch your fingers, this machine bites! He had lost his fingers trying to pull the paper out slower than the machine was going and slipped as the blade came down to cut the next page. It's not that I am into the elderly, but I love hanging out with mature men. It's a selfish thing; I want to learn from their mistakes! The example of those who have gone through life is precious and can teach us so much if we take the time to listen and once we listen, it's our turn to teach those who come up behind us. Let's hope the lessons we share aren't the same ones that they shared with us, unless we learned from them and are wiser for it! What are we passing on to the next generation? A simple question but so important.

Peace,
Tom

ISAIAH 30:21

Your ears will hear a word behind you,
"This is the way, walk in it,"
whenever you turn to the right or to the left.

Shhhhh…can you hear it…there it is again…quiet…close your mind to all the sounds of this busy world in which we live and sit there quietly for a moment…can you hear it now…I wonder what you thought at you read the beginning lines for today…did we hear anything as we sat quietly…listening? Maybe some of you thought there was going to be a big bang…or maybe some music to go along with the reading - nope - I wanted us to take a moment and listen - listen for the voice of God in a small whisper - sometimes we may not hear Him because we never take the time to listen…so try it now again - sit quietly and see if you can hear Him - the voice of our Father in heaven whispering to us…I wonder what He is saying to you…

Peace,
Tom

PSALM 25:9

He leads the humble in justice,
and He teaches the humble His way.

It had happened many years before, when I was a fairly new driver… I was driving down my street behind a neighbor, we came to the intersection, as I watched, he drove out into traffic and out of nowhere another car came and hit him broadside…I had two options… drive right past or stop and help…I was late for an appointment so the urge was to leave…I thought to myself, someone else will stop… there were other drivers around…but then I heard His Voice… "go and help". My neighbor wasn't someone who I had gotten to know in the neighborhood - sure I had seen him here and there and even delivered papers to his house when I was younger…but stopping and helping made the difference that years later he never forgot. He had commented to my parents many times about the time I stopped and helped. Listening for God's whispers can have an effect for years to come…we will have to humble ourselves to hear what is He whispering to us…what is He asking you to do for Him today, …

Peace,
Tom

HEBREWS 12:25

See to it that you do not refuse Him who is speaking.
For if those did not escape when they
refused him who warned them on earth,
much less will we escape who turn away from Him
who warns from heaven.

As a house fire burns, it begins to eat up all the oxygen and the thick black smoke begins to bank down until there is total darkness… being only able to see about 2 inches in front of your face, firefighters must find the fire in order to put it out. With nothing to see but black and feeling around as you bump into this piece of furniture and that, groping along the walls, you can get a little turned around and not be able to find the seat of the fire. If you stop moving around, take a moment, stop your breathing - you can "hear" the crackling of the fire - it is only like a whisper - you need to listen close or you won't hear it and if you don't hear it you will go around aimlessly. Today's verse shares about not refusing Him who speaks and warns from Heaven. Sometimes in our life, things can seem to go black - we have lost the "oxygen" to keep going, we seem to be going in circles with no clear direction - it is then that we must stop, take a moment and listen - listen for the whisper of His Voice and once we hear it - we need to follow it or run the risk of going aimlessly in life… are we listening for His Whisper today…

Peace,
Tom

GALATIANS 5:16

But I say, walk by the Spirit,
and you will not carry out the desire of the flesh.

I love the mornings… each morning Dee, our family dog, and I talk a walk - whether it's in the flowery morning of spring, or the heat of a summer morning or the crunchy leafs of fall or in the deep new snow that has fallen through the night - we walk. Why some ask - well for me it is in the quietness of those mornings that I can separate the noise of life, of my own thoughts to hear the whispers of God…

it's quiet and that means all the distractions of life seem a little less overpowering and I can ask - did God say that? - a time to separate the "my thoughts" from His Words to me - no I don't hear an audible voice but I can feel His Whisper in my heart...and it's nice to take the time to walk with Him before the business of the day comes upon me...and then I end the day with prayer with my wife - a time to let God hear our whispers of prayers and hopes and dreams...when do you take time to hear the whispers of God...

Peace,
Tom

JOHN 14:26

But the Helper, the Holy Spirit,
whom the Father will send in My name,
He will teach you all things,
and bring to your remembrance all that I said to you.

After an accident during my time on the fire department, I had to get hearing aids. One of the things I miss most since getting them is the whispers of my wife as we fall asleep together - you see every night I take the hearing aids out and for the most part I cannot hear her whispers to me...don't get me wrong, I am so blessed to be able to hear what I can with the hearing aids but hearing the whispers of the one you love is... well something special. I am glad though I do not need my hearing aids to hear the whispers of my God who loves me. He loves you too and wants nothing more than to whisper to your heart just how much He loves you. A great place to start is for us to be quiet for a moment...to tune everything else out and just sit and listen... He will speak to you - He will share what He has planned for you, the great adventures that await...He will say "I love you!" - it's never too late...have a quiet moment with God and hear what He whispers to you...

Peace,
Tom

EPHESIANS 2:14

For He Himself is our peace,
who made both groups into one
and broke down the barrier of the dividing wall

Today, we will devote ourselves to breaking down the walls that separate us on this earth , walls that keep us from truly loving each other…I remember one night in the fire house, when the subject of the young man who my daughter was dating came up - you see he was an African American and some of the "white" guys could not understand how I would allow that - I asked a simple question to them - would it be better if she dated a white guy who beat her tor an African American who would treat her right?" The sad reality was that their answer was the white guy… it is this kind of thinking and living that causes us to shake our head but it shouldn't end there - we need to have restored relationships with those we have fallen away from and a great one to start is with Jesus …how about it - why not restore your relationship with Him today or better yet start one!

Peace,
Tom

MATTHEW 5:44

But I say to you,
love your enemies and pray for those who persecute you,

As an officer in the fire department, you have to deal with men who sometimes try your patience…whether they disagreed with what you thought was the correct action to take or one that came to work under the influence. When I first made lieutenant, I was assigned to a fire house where one of the men came to work drunk - not falling down drunk but drunk enough to cause problems - most guys would look the other way but I could not - I needed to address the situation the first day I saw it - it obviously caused problems - the man didn't understand why I was "picking" on him - I tried to explain that it was for his own good…each time he showed up for work in that condition, I would call the chief and send him home. During the days when he came in not under the influence, I would try to talk with him about

51

his drinking - well over time, he left my crew - I had often prayed for him to come to a place of understanding…well years later at a bible study - who do you think showed up…yep - it was that guy from years before and one of the first things he said to me what " thanks for trying to help me back then - I never forgot what you said to me - I have been sober for over four years now" - those words made me feel glad that I had never turned my head from the problem like so many others - he in fact said that the conversations we had on the good days led him to take a good look at himself and eventually led him to get help… reconciliation can take many forms in our life and they all deal with a transfusion of hope…where does hope need to be applied in your life…

Peace,
Tom

EPHESIANS 4:2

*"with all humility and gentleness, with patience,
showing tolerance for one another in love,"*

Spending time thinking of reconciliation, I remembered when I was a small child - on the way home from school, we used to walk past this five and dime store - there along the counter were jars filled with candy and I remember one time going in with some of the others who were walking home… some purchased things but I was one who gently lifted the lid and grabbed a whole hand full of candy…when I got home, I remember my parents had found the candy and made me go back the next day to return it and pay for what I had taken, I also had to say I was sorry to the owner. I was blessed to have parents who taught me about reconciliation - admitting when we had failed and making it right - the great thing about inviting Jesus in is that we admit we have sinned but He has made all things right by going to the Cross for each of us - when we come to realize the full nature of the Cross, we are living in the good news of reconciliation…so I ask - have we been to the Cross lately…

Peace,
Tom

JOHN 13:35

"By this all men will know that you are My disciples,
if you have love for one another."

It was late one night in the fire house when another fire fighter and I began a discussion that opened my eyes to something that I knew was true but never had the occasion to speak about it with an African American - the other fire fighter and I had come on together and had not only a working relationship but a friendship had developed as well and as he and I began to speak of the prejudice that exists in the world today, we began to speak of how he felt about it - he shared with me that deep in his heart, he held all white people guilty of how he was and is treated as an African American - he said "you and I can go into a store together - you dress in rags and me dress in a suit coat and the store owner will follow me around the store just because of the color of my skin..." He went on to say "this is true in most cases because of the deep seated feelings that people have because of what they have heard or read without giving it a second thought" - wow - to be judged base on skin color or any other differences not only hurts the one judging but hurts the one being judged to the point of changing their perspective because of that judgment...we need to stop judging based upon skin color or other physical differences and begin loving base upon Jesus and it can start with us...because believe it or not - we are all different in some way...

Peace,
Tom

PSALM 133:1

Behold, how good and how pleasant it is
For brothers to dwell together in unity!

Reconciliation and living in the good news of it, means speaking up when there are injustices done. Growing up, I am sure we all have seen an injustice done just because someone was different, not like the "so called normal" people. Whenever I think of that, Dave comes to mind - a boy who was born with a challenging mental condition - some called him retarded or an idiot but my mom and dad took the time to befriend him in our neighborhood, when most turned a blind eye or even worse made fun of him - even today I can be sitting at my parent's house and the phone will ring and it will be Dave - just calling to say hello and maybe talk awhile. That's all he was looking for in life - someone to share in his life - a friendly voice to say hello - most will never know the uniqueness of Dave because of some inner sense that they are somehow better than him…we, who know Jesus, need never to refuse to be quiet in sharing the love of Christ - especially to those who are "different" than ourselves…come to think of it - we all are different and I bet Jesus never even thought about that as He hung on the Cross for us…so are we living in the good news of reconciliation…are we refusing to be quiet-

Peace,
Tom

PROVERBS 3:21-22

²¹ My son, let them not vanish from your sight;
Keep sound wisdom and discretion,
²² So they will be life to your soul
And adornment to your neck.

I am sure you may have heard that old saying "your eyes are the windows to your soul"! It may seem strange to us men to have someone tell us what movies we should or should not be watching, and the reality is that we ourselves should hold a standard in our own life as to what is acceptable to watch…I remember the first movie I ever went to see - my grandmother took my brother and I to see Mary Poppins. I remember as she walked us in, got our tickets and sat back to watch the big screen - the movie was so pure and innocent to a child of about five years old, but now I have to say that I haven't been to see a movie in quite a while - the purity and innocence seems to be gone… there is a standard that I try to hold as I watch any media - can Jesus sit next to me as I watch it…what standard do you hold as you watch…

Peace,
Tom

JOHN 17:15-16

¹⁵ I do not ask You to take them out of the world,
but to keep them from the evil one.
¹⁶ They are not of the world,
even as I am not of the world.

Okay now be honest... how many of us haven't passed a sign that said "WET PAINT" and not wanted to reach out to see if it is really wet? There's just something about our manly nature that makes us want to reach out and touch it - or how about passing an accident... slowing down to see what we can see... way back in the Garden, we all fell away from God when Adam and Eve choose to believe the lie...because of their choice, we, men, have within us an evil nature, but the key is whether we want to choose to live in that evil nature... there is the old adage that your eyes are the windows to your soul - think about it - we can look into a person's eyes and see if they are having a bad day or a good day...we, ourselves, can choose by what we see with our eyes, to allow good or bad into our souls...it comes down to choice...what are we allowing into our souls this day...

Peace,
Tom

COLOSSIANS 4:5-6

⁵ Conduct yourselves with wisdom toward outsiders,
making the most of the opportunity.
⁶ Let your speech always be with grace,
as though seasoned with salt,
so that you will know how you should respond to each person.

I wonder...would we stand by and watch a person get beaten, or shot, or robbed, or possibly even raped or a couple engage in a sexual embrace ...would we stand idle as it happened right in front of us...I think not and yet so often the movies that we watch have those scenes with in them. Don't get me wrong, all movies are not bad but some of them cross the line...what line you may ask - the line drawn by the Word of God. We need to follow the standards that are set in God's Word, we need to be men of action - standing up for the biblical standards that God has laid before us - there needs to be a difference between what Christians watch and what the world watches - we should be setting the standard so I ask - when was the last time you walked out of a movie because of a graphic scene or situation…not caring about how much money we spent to watch it but caring more about the line that was crossed in the film…and not be afraid to tell others how we truly felt about a movie when asked…are we willing to cross the line drawn in the sand to stand up for Truth…what culture are we engaging in - one that stands for God or one that stands for the world's view…tough questions deserving tough answers…

Peace,
Tom

COLOSSIANS 2:8

See to it that no one takes you captive
through philosophy and empty deception,
according to the tradition of men,
according to the elementary principles of the world,
rather than according to Christ.

Back in high school, I took this class on Media and its effects on the human race. One part of it dealt with subliminal advertisement - I am sure you heard about how there was a time when the movie producers would put little clips of dry deserts to sell more drinks in the concession stand or pictures of hot steamy popcorn - people would make purchases based upon this subliminal advertisement without really ever knowing it was happening to them. Movies today can have the same effect - you see movies are packed with meaning and sometimes we are not ever aware that there is a hidden agenda - those messages can be both good and bad - like "The Lion, Witch and the Wardrobe" or "The Golden Compass" - within each of these movies are hidden agendas - the question then remains - do we understand the full reaching effects of the movies we watch… are we catching the hidden meaning in what we are watching… today's verse speaks to us about not letting anyone take you captive through philosophy and empty deception… are you being deceived by the world or are we living with our eyes open to the Truth…

Peace,
Tom

MATTHEW 5:13

"You are the salt of the earth;
but if the salt has become tasteless,
how can it be made salty again?
It is no longer good for anything,
except to be thrown out and trampled underfoot by men.

What are we watching with our eyes... what is the standard we use when watching different media? I took a moment the other day to look through some of the DVD's that we have at my home. You know the ones your children give you for gifts, ones that we have purchased to watch and I came across a copy of a movie that I would say is my favorite - it is not entertaining but it is enlightening - it is of course The Passion of The Christ by Mel Gibson. If you have never seen it, I would encourage you to watch it. It truly shows the love of our Heavenly Father and gift of Jesus Christ to each of us. It can be a difficult movie to watch for the scenes are very graphic but it does not hold a candle to what actually happened to our Brother, our Savior Jesus, as He became our sin. If He could do that for us, don't you think we could make sure what we choose in our media is according to God's Standards for His People... I pray that we all make godly choices in our movie selections and what we allow into our souls through our eyes.

Peace,
Tom

PSALM 1:1-2

[1] How blessed is the man who does not walk
in the counsel of the wicked,
Nor stand in the path of sinners,
Nor sit in the seat of scoffers!
[2] But his delight is in the law of the Lord,
And in His law he meditates day and night.

Once again God brings to my life something of meaning that seems to match the theme of my devotions... I, myself, am not a hunter but anyone who enjoys the outdoors will be able to grasp the meaning of today's devotion. I am a fisherman and during the winter months in Buffalo NY, we take to the ice…I happened to be out with a few men on Saturday as we took to the ice for a bit of outdoor fun. What occurred to me, as we sat and waited for the fish to bite, was that as other men came to where we were fishing, to ask if we were catching anything and to see what type of bait we were using, all but two of the men who approached used profane language in sharing about ice fishing. They were throwing around words that well let's just say were offensive to me and the others around me…as each of them left, the group I was with, commented at how it was sad that within all the beauty that surrounded us, these men needed to use vulgarity to get their message across…one man even said "Holy" - we commented to each other how could he ever associate those two words together … we did not let those men affect the beauty of spending time in one of God's wonders…but we didn't go far enough as men who follow Christ, we needed to speak up and let them know the language was offensive…we needed to find the strength in Christ and each other to delight in the law of the Lord…

Peace,
Tom

PSALM 37:5

Commit your way to the Lord,
Trust also in Him, and He will do it.

Each of us have a choice - I believe it's the second greatest thing God gave us (the first of course being Jesus and the plan of redemption) a free choice to live the way WE want - sometimes the decisions that we make can be hurtful to others - sometimes they may not understand - a few years ago, I took a walk over to my neighbor Fred's - you see it was his birthday - he was 99 years old - yes I said 99 - we talked for a while - Fred is in great shape - still drives and gets about - he told me that he is slowing down a little but I told him that's to be expected - I mean he is one year away from 100.. and then we got to the discussion (one that we have often) I said Fred - do you believe in God and that He sent Jesus to go to the cross for us - to show us His Love .. and Fred's choice was .. no - he just doesn't believe that - he has his own thoughts on the subject - and as I eventually walked home

I couldn't help but think that in all of Fred's years on this earth and the things that he has seen and done and the people he has met- he has not experienced the love of God in a real and personal way - I was sadden by his choice and will continue to witness to him - I would like to see him get to know my friend Jesus someday but.. it's his choice.. what are we choosing today..

Peace,

Tom

REVELATION 5:9

And they sang a new song, saying,
"Worthy are You to take the book and to break its seals;
for You were slain, and purchased for God with Your blood
men from every tribe and tongue and people and nation.

Many nights at the firehouse were spent sharing a meal together - sometimes before we finished the meal - we would get a fire call - it would end up being a "working" fire - that meant that we did what we always did and ran into a burning building to save life, save property and keep each other safe - the amazing thing about it all was that whether we were sharing a meal or fighting the fire - the color of our skin or the background of where we came from was never an issue - now not all firehouses acted in the same manner and too often we see that kind of prejudice displayed throughout life - some will only share with those of the "same" background or skin color .. let us be reminded of an old saying that heard again recently and found amusing but true .. when it comes right down to it.. we are all members of the "Adams Family" - remember that show - "their creepy and their spooky - their altogether kooky .. - we all have our beginning with a God who created us as His People .. maybe we should try and treat each other that way.. members of His Family, some just don't know it yet!

Peace,

Tom

1 THESSALONIANS 5:11

Therefore,
encourage one another and build up one another,
just as you also are doing.

I recently spent a day helping my daughter and son - in - law as they build their new house, we were putting up 8x8 columns and other beams to form the entrance way to their new home, later that same evening, I had the privilege of officiating the marriage of a couple who were starting out on their journey together and at the close of the day, I thought to myself how building a house takes lots of hard work, sweat and vision, and I thought how building a home takes the same if not more hard work, sweat and vision but the key to both building a house and building a home is exactly that, building and working together, encouraging each other, making positive progression each day, a simple little comment like "I do" can go a long way whether your agreeing to share life, or encouraging a loved one or even a total stranger, so why not help someone out today by sharing an encouraging word! Hope you are encouraged today for God loves you!

Peace,
Tom

PHILIPPIANS 1:6

For I am confident of this very thing,
that He who began a good work in you
will perfect it until the day of Christ Jesus.

As a young boy, I never would have imagined that the lessons learned by playing with my toys would give me the knowledge I have today. I started out playing with Tinker Toys, little sticks and plastic and wooden pieces used to build things; you could let your imagination run wild! I then graduated to Lincoln Logs and built many log cabins, and then I was finally old enough and had learned the basics of how to build things, my dad brought out his erector set and the possibilities were endless of what I could build, it had motors and cranks, nuts and bolts. I can still recall the first time I opened the box, we may not know just what the Lord has in store for us as we start off with just the small things in life but I know, based upon today's scripture, that He will be perfecting us as we learn to keep building upon a good foundation! Today due to the Tinker Toys, Lincoln Logs and the erector set, I can build a house, imagine what God is building through us... just imagine, the possibilities are endless!

Peace,
Tom

LUKE 6:48

"he is like a man building a house,
who dug deep and laid a foundation on the rock;
and when a flood occurred,
the torrent burst against that house and could not shake it,
because it had been well built."

Night after night, he went out and then early the next morning he went back out to cover up his nights work... I remember as a young boy, spending hours skating on our back yard ice rink, the hours of fun, the games of hockey, the memories are still strong in my mind but it was only recently that I became aware of the hours my dad spent putting water on the frozen ground to make that ice rink, night after night, he spent hours watering the snow until it started to freeze, each layer of ice building upon the next. I remember him saying that for the ice rink to be strong enough to skate on, it needed a good foundation and to protect what the night freeze had done, he would go out in the morning and put snow on the ice to protect it from the sun's heat of the day. For us to have strong faith we need to build upon a good foundation, we need to go on building that foundation day and night, for protection from the attacks of Satan, to have the faith to stand strong when temptation comes. The question is when was the last time you watered your faith?

Peace,
Tom

ISAIAH 61:7

Instead of your shame there shall be a double portion;
instead of dishonor they shall rejoice in their lot;
therefore in their land they shall possess a double portion;
they shall have everlasting joy.

There was shame and dishonor when I heard those words that no son ever wants to hear "Tom, you disappointed me! Those words came from the lips of my father, someone who I hold in high esteem. I had once again let him down due to my anger and it was a family gathering when my anger, when I lost control and in my rage hurt those I love, not physically, thank God, but sometimes words hurt more than physical pain. Come to think of it, I am not really sure what it was all about but I will never forget the look on his face and those words that cut me to the core. I needed to change my behavior, I needed to act my age, and toddlers have tantrums not young men! I needed to bring him honor like today's verse states. I thank God I find the strength in my Heavenly Father to bring honor to my earthly father. Have you disappointed anyone and need to make a change? Turn to God, cry out to Him, He is there to help!

Peace,
Tom

1 CORINTHIANS 14:26

What is the outcome then, brethren?
When you assemble, each one has a psalm,
has a teaching, has a revelation, has a tongue,
has an interpretation. Let all things be done for edification.

Put tab A into slot B, followed by putting tab C into slot D, at first glance I wasn't sure exactly what the plans meant but as I examine each piece it began to take shape. With each step followed exactly as it was written, the bookcase seemed to come to life. But to be honest, there was a time there when I just couldn't figure out what they were asking. By the time I had glued board W to side board X, I thought I was going crazy and the frustration grew, I knew I had to slow down and take each step in order to finish the project. Sometimes in life, we need to slow down, re read the manual of life (AKA The Bible) and make sure we have followed the plans step by step to accomplish what He has in store for us, sure we may get frustrated at times, when life doesn't seem to be going our way but then again, is it about us or about Him? His finished projects are so much better than ours! Then next time we find ourselves getting frustrated, let's ask ourselves is it about us or Him?

Peace,
Tom

JOHN 10:10

The thief comes only to steal and kill and destroy;
I came that they may have life, and have it abundantly.

There is an old story of this young couple who comes to their pastor and asks him to pray for God's blessing upon them...the pastor asks if they are married - they reply no, we are living together... his response is ...than I cannot pray for you...the young couple is dismayed at the pastors answer...why not they ask...he says to them "how can we ask God to bless you both when you are living in sin". It may seem that the pastor is hard and not very understanding but the reality of the situation is that the pastor spoke the truth - we cannot ask God to bless sin - but the story doesn't end there - the pastor offers a room in his house for the man to live in while the couple makes plans and takes premarital classes. The man agrees and begins a six month journey to get their lives in a God honoring relationship with his soon to be wife - at the wedding, the pastor takes the couple aside and says "now I will ask for God's blessing upon you!" - we need to make sure that our spiritual wheel is in line with God, so often we cry out to God for this and that without first examining where we are in our relationship to living the Gospel...healthy through and through starts and ends with our spiritual walk...I wonder, is our spiritual wheel a little flat and in need of some fresh Air...

Peace,
Tom

PROVERBS 10:28

The hope of the righteous is gladness,
But the expectation of the wicked perishes.

Sad to say, sometimes our children have seen the ugly side of life… you know the times that show the struggles of this life, even sadder the times when our humanness has gotten in the way of our walk, but I also believe they have seen the goodness of the transforming power of Jesus Christ in our lives as well. If you were to ask my daughters to describe me, I am sure they would say that there are times when their dad was not exactly acting like he should…but they would also say there are times when he acts crazy, foolish, funny. I pray that they know that it is Christ who brings me joy, happiness and also helps me through the struggles. I never hid the fact that we are growing into what Christ wants us to be - godly, caring people and that we should try to live Christ always and recognize that there are times when we fail but also recognize the tremendous love and forgiveness our Heavenly Father has for us…much like the love and forgiveness that we need to share with each other. Loving God truly is enjoying life - the ups and the downs but trying to find the peace through it all… what are you trying to do as you love God and enjoy life…

Peace,
Tom

DEUTERONOMY 16:14

and you shall rejoice in your feast,
you and your son and your daughter
and your male and female servants
and the Levite and the stranger and the orphan
and the widow who are in your towns.

As many of you know, I volunteered as the New York AG Western Section Men's Ministry leader and one of the most asked questions by wives is "how do we get men in our churches?". It is a question that is asked by many - not only wives but pastors as well. Back when I was pastoring a church in Lackawanna NY, one of the ways we got men to come to church was having a "game night". It was a night of playing games…ping pong, air hockey, pool and there were board games there as well for those who would rather just sit and play. We offered free pizza and wings and snacks. The nights were well attended and everyone seemed to have a good time but the best part of the night for me was when I would notice one or two of the men would seem to go missing…looking for them to make sure things were okay, I would always find them in the sanctuary. Sometimes one man would be sharing with others and sometimes the men would gather there just to pray. I guess you could say it was "Holy Pleasure" …what holy pleasure do you have in your life?

Peace,
Tom

JOHN 1:1

In the beginning was the Word,
and the Word was with God,
and the Word was God.

Whether I was building a new house for a customer, or starting a garden in the yard, or building a new relationship, I found that I had to start with the basics. When building a house, the foundation needed to be right, with a garden, I had to remove everything from the soil that was not good for growing, and in a relationship, it had to be built on truth. I've had my share of bad beginnings but when I started with the basics, took care to be sure they were started right, houses were built true and square, gardens had plenty of harvest and friendships still last today. As we walk through this thing called life, we should start building upon a good foundation and today's scripture is the best place to start. " In the beginning was the Word, and the Word was with God and the Word was God" If we try to start anywhere else, it will lead to building up something other than the Truth! We can start anytime, anyplace, at any age, so why not put down your phone, turn off the TV and open the Bible - you will begin a journey that will flourish like nothing you ever imagined!

Peace,
Tom

1 PETER 1:18-19

*[18] "Knowing that you were not redeemed
with perishable things like silver or gold
from your futile way of life
inherited from your forefathers,
[19] but with precious blood,
as of a lamb unblemished and spotless,
the blood of Christ."*

Many times I have fallen away from a chance to share Christ - it is not something I am proud of or even like to share - there were times when I knew that I would face ridicule, be labeled as one of "those" and I fell - I fell to the lie of Satan that I should care more about myself than my God or the fact of what others thought of me was somehow so much more important than what God had asked me to do and I have to wonder today   - was my sharing Christ the last chance they had to receive Him as Lord and Savior.. did they die shortly after I was supposed to share with them - you know in a freak accident of some sort or maybe their heart just gave out - in either case I could sit and let that thought keep me deep in depression but life with Christ never ends there - you see I wake each day and realize that today is a new day and that if given the opportunity to share I jump at the chance - no matter where, no matter with who and not because I think I have to .. .I want to! I want others to know what I know - that I have the best friend a guy could ask for - He never lets me down and is always there to talk with and no matter how many times I fall short - He still loves me. And He loves you too but we should be about His Business of sharing Him… so when was the last time you shared Him?

Peace,
Tom

PHILIPPIANS 1:11

*"Having been filled with the fruit of righteousness
which comes through Jesus Christ,
to the glory and praise of God."*

When I used to frame houses and had to build walls - we had

to make sure they were square - so we went to the standard or rule that says 3 feet on one side and 4 feet on the other would equal 5 feet across both points - it was and is called the 3,4,5 rule (or for the guys who like big words, the Pythagorean theorem) - you may be asking what this has to do with today's scripture readings- well at the end of each day we should pray that our life is "squaring" up - and the rule we need to use is Jesus - plain and simple - no big formulas or equations - just Jesus - do we measure up.. I am not sure where you are when you read these but those living in the Buffalo, NY area got a taste of some terrific wind - as I was out in it today - I could only imagine what it must have been like in the room when the Holy Spirit came upon the disciples - for in Acts it says that a noise like a violent, rushing wind filled the house and they received power - that same power is available to us to help us be filled with the fruit of righteousness.. the question is, are we square with Jesus…

Peace,
Tom

ROMANS 8:28

And we know that God causes all things to work together
for good to those who love God,
to those who are called according to His purpose.

My plan was to have a wonderful time, but it rained! One of my nephews was moving out of the area and I wanted to go fishing with him before he was to leave, so we set the date, and no sooner had we arrived at my favorite fishing hole, when the rain came and came hard. We were going to try and stick it out but the weather had turned worse with each passing minute so we headed back to shore, trailering the boat home, we notice the weather seemed to change so we pulled into another spot and fished from shore. No sooner did we have our lines in the water, the sky cracked with thunder and the rains came again, so we packed up and headed home. I felt bad that we didn't have a chance to fish together, to talk awhile but as we turned for home, we saw the sun come out, so we stopped at another spot and we fished and talked he even caught a good size fish among other the other fish we caught. We had a night of it and have some great memories! Sometimes in life, our plans don't always go as planned.

Things seem to get in the way or stop our plans from unfolding as we want but as today's verse states, we can know for sure that God causes all things to work together for good. We never would have caught the fish we did, or have that last great time together if we gave up! He is in control! We just have to let go of the reins and keep trying! Don't give up today, He isn't!

Peace,
Tom

JEREMIAH 29:11

For I know the plans that I have for you,
declares the Lord,
plans for welfare and not for calamity
to give you a future and a hope.

While climbing around in the attic of our garage, I happened to see them and I sat there for a moment, a little disappointed. Getting something for one of my daughters in the attic, I ran across my old firefighting turnout gear, it still had the smell of the fires I had fought in them. I thought about the men and woman who I worked with, braved the infernos with, ready to lay down my life with, the time my dad and I delivered a baby, the many people I helped on first aid call. And to be honest, I felt disappointed that my career was cut short. I knew if I stayed there long enough, and kept thinking the way I was, the disappointment would have over whelmed me, so I turned away and happened to glance down at the work bench, there sat one of my Bibles (yes I keep a Bible on my workbench - you never know when you might want to give it a read!) and I said thank you God, not only for seeing the Bible but realizing that without leaving the fire dept. I would not have met the many friends, and godly men along this journey - a journey of a future and of hope, so don't sit too long in disappointment, come to realize that God has plans for you that you never thought existed!

Peace,
Tom

PSALM 23:1

The Lord is my shepherd, I shall not want.

It was a good twenty minutes as I watched my dad fight the huge musky that had taken his lure, and as each passing minute went by I found myself more and more excited for him, but it was not always that way. When I was a young boy, my dad took my brother and I fishing and as that day went on, my brother caught all the fish; little ones, big ones, even a golden carp that we kept in a tank for many years - needless to say, I was very disappointed that day, that I didn't catch any fish but he did. One of the lessons to come out of that day where my brother caught all the fish was my dad sharing with me about being happy that someone caught fish, and it didn't have to be me! So fast forward to the musky, and I remembered those words my father shared so long ago. Here I was learning from my disappointment and enjoying that someone else was catching a fish and what a fish it was, a huge musky! Living life will have those disappointing days, but learning from them, learning not to want, like today's scripture shares, the Lord is my shepherd, I shall not want, can make the difference between staying disappointed or enjoying a beautiful memory!

Peace,
Tom

PSALM 42:11

Why are you in despair, O my soul?
And why have you become disturbed within me?
Hope in God, for I shall yet praise Him,
The help of my countenance and my God.

I wish I had one more day, one more hour, one minute more, some disappointment will never truly be gone from our lives, we will live with that pain. I wish I had one more day with my mom. One more opportunity to tell her I love her, one more hour to sit with her, one more minute to hold her hand but sometimes the life of those we love comes to an end here on earth and the disappointments will be carried quietly in our hearts. Today's verse shares, we can have hope in God and that's a good thing, a great thing for I know I will see her again one day standing in heaven! I can learn from that disappointment by making today count! So can you, don't let today become a disappointment in what we will wish we had done when tomorrow comes, do it today, just love those around us for we never know when it will be the last day, hour or minute with them!

Peace,
Tom

JOHN 13:35

*"By this all men will know that you are My disciples,
if you have love for one another."*

It's not about us; a good friend reminded me of this. There are times when we must leave a church, my friend suggested that we not use the term "leave" but use the word "transfer" for the work of the Lord continues. He was right - you see many years ago, I had to leave, I mean transfer from one church to another - it was a difficult decision - I had many friends and coworkers of His Kingdom there - there were memories of great times - of moves of the Spirit - there were even tears along the way , as in all church communities but in the end I had to face either the loyalty to man or the loyalty to God - I could have stayed but I would have made it about me and that is not what Christ is all about - it is about serving others and so I made the decision to "transfer" to where I felt God calling - - - you see I learned that Church was not about me but about Him .. I pray as we engage in the community of Christ, no matter where we find ourselves fellowshipping, we view Church as not about ourselves but about being the "ultimate witness" to those who do not know our Savior Jesus Christ - may you spend time in a Christ centered church where He calls you to

Peace,
Tom

1 THESSALONIANS 5:14

We urge you, brethren, admonish the unruly,
encourage the fainthearted,
help the weak, be patient with everyone.

I heard two messages recently about sharing Christ - both preachers I heard spoke of getting outside of ourselves and sharing Christ - it is easier, you know, to sit back and be served than it is to go out and serve others but that is not what Jesus did - He lived His life serving those around Him and even today - as He sits in glory, He sits there as our advocate, on our behalf. Have we ever thought about going outside our comfort zone to those in need - we can all make excuses to sit and stay comfortable but that's not what He has called us to.. I'll never forget the story my dad told me one time - He was at work at the firehouse, when a man came in and needed to use the bathroom - so my dad showed him and the man asked if my dad could help him - you see this man had no arms - my dad helped him - and it is here that I began to understand how far we must go to help others - my dad shared more than most would have that day and I know he did it for what Christ has done for him - I wonder how far are we willing to go or do for Christ..

Peace,
Tom

PROVERBS 4:1-2

¹ Hear, O sons, the instruction of a father,
And give attention that you may gain understanding,
² for I give you sound teaching;
Do not abandon my instruction.

You paid for the whole hammer didn't you? Words that my father in law, a master carpenter, had said to me when we were working together at putting a deck together. I wasn't sure what he meant by that so I had to ask. He repeated what he said, "you paid for the whole hammer didn't you?" I replied yes, he then went on to say, well why not use the whole hammer Tom, your using only part of the handle, slide your hand down to the end of the handle and try hitting the nails now! As I tried it, I learned that it took less strength to drive the nails in; less stress on my elbow and forearm it was a valuable lesson learned. We must be willing to learn from those who have gone before us, to learn not only the secrets to driving nails or other lessons but also in life. Today's scripture shares a great point that seems to be lost in today's day and age. We should give attention so that we may gain understanding! Why not listen to those who have gone before us. They want to share it with us, the question is are we listening and why not listen to another Carpenter!

Peace,
Tom

1 THESSALONIANS 4:3

For this is the will of God, your sanctification;
that is, that you abstain from sexual immorality;

I am not sure how old I was but I remember not being able to wait to be old enough to ride a ride at a local amusement park... the ride was one where you could actually drive a motorcar. The cars ran on a track with a metal brace that kept the cars from going off the track. You really didn't have to drive them - you could have just sat there and eventually you would have ended up back at the starting line but as a little kid, I didn't know that - I thought that I was actually driving and it fascinated me and couldn't wait to be old enough to ride it...well when the year came and I got to drive, I remember how hard it was to keep the car on the right path...if I didn't hold on to the wheel with all that I had, the car would veer off to one side and then BANG - it hit the metal bar that kept the car on the track. I remember trying over and over to make it around the whole track without hitting the bar...it was almost impossible - you see the pathway to drive around the whole track was hard and it took all that I had...much like the "pathway for holiness" in our walk to remain sexually pure...a lot of hard work to keep the steering straight and stay on course...I wonder if we have fallen off the track recently and need to grab a hold of the wheel with both hands and steer straight ahead...

Peace,
Tom

2 CORINTHIANS 10:5

*We are destroying speculations and every lofty thing
raised up against the knowledge of God,
and we are taking every thought captive
to the obedience of Christ*

The reality is that God made women beautiful to men...the question that arises is when we look at women, do we see the outer beauty or the inner and which is more important. For me personally and the struggle to stay a man of purity comes from few different places. I have read many books where I learned the technique of bouncing away from something that I knew would entice me and the other came from the realization that every woman is someone's mother or sister or daughter and how would I like it if someone looked at my mother or sister or daughters with lust in their heart. Being a father of three daughters has opened my eyes to a lot. When we are walking somewhere and my daughters are in front of me, I can see the "fellas" trying to take a good look (if you know what I mean) therefore it strengths my desire to stay pure and to have them dress appropriately at all times...little tools to help me make the right choice...what tools are you using to take every thought captive to the obedience of Christ?

Peace,
Tom

PHILIPPIANS 4:8

*Finally, brethren, whatever is true,
whatever is honorable, whatever is right,
whatever is pure, whatever is lovely,
whatever is of good repute,
if there is any excellence and if anything worthy of praise,
dwell on these things.*

It starts with one look and then a desire to see more...I bet when you read that, you immediately thought I was speaking of looking at a women or man in an unholy way but what if our initial thought was one of reading God's Word...you see that's how sin takes a hold of us and gets us to think one thing when it could be something entirely different. Over the years I have had the opportunity to ask men what their biggest problem is in walking the walk and without a doubt it's usually the same answer…pornography, of some sort, has crept into their lives and found a home…being with fire fighters, men who show "true masculinity", seem to somehow get drawn into that bad place - they wear a patch on their shoulder that says "that others may live" but forget sometimes that being truly masculine is having the ability to ask for help when the battle becomes too bad…sometimes short circuiting porn's power means admitting we need help…do we need to take the first step and ask for help… if we are going to live today's scripture, we need to make sure that we are walking by the Spirit with a little help from other men who have gone down that path.

Peace,
Tom

EPHESIANS 4:29

Let no unwholesome word proceed from your mouth,
but only such a word as is good for edification
according to the need of the moment,
so that it will give grace to those who hear.

I will never forget the time, many years ago, when I heard a father call their child "stupid" in a group setting - the father continued it for years - and as I look back and look at the child today, they have grown up with very low self - esteem problems and many issues that seem to stem from hearing they were "stupid". They had in fact grown up to be stupid in their own eyes. I am using that word only because that was the word I heard the child use to describe them self. I personally do not believe that anyone is stupid but if told enough times a person, as in this case, comes to believe what they are told. I wonder .. if that parent had told their child that they were the best and the brightest, regardless of their difficulties, what would be that child's opinion of themselves today.. we never really think about the damage we can do to someone else in how we relate to them .. I wonder if we, men, took Paul's advice to the Ephesians (today's key bible verse) in how we speak, how many of the downtrodden today would be edified.. how many of our marriages would be filled with love…how many of our children would grow up to be emotionally healthy.. maybe we should start liberating others with our words of wholesome talk..

Peace,
Tom

PROVERBS 16:24

"Pleasant words are a honeycomb,
Sweet to the soul and healing to the bones."

Ever thought about a husband's sacrifice play - I began to think about the "sacrifice" play - you know the one in baseball where the batter gives up his chance to go around the bases to score so that another can make it home. Jesus gave up His life so we can make it home and it was done because of LOVE. I thought to myself "am I willing to give up my chance at bat so that another can make it home?" - I pray that I will always give that up for my wife but it shouldn't end there .. it should be not only for her but anyone. Today's verse speaks of pleasant words are a honeycomb, sweet to the soul and healing to the bones, I wonder how our words are to others, are they a comfort or do they bring division? When I was a firefighter, we wore a patch on our arms that had the Latin words "ut vavant alli" - it stood for "that others may live" - those are some good words to use in how a good Christian should live.. for others - I pray that we examined who we walk for .. ourselves or others in the name of Christ ..

Peace,
Tom

ROMANS 12:12

rejoicing in hope,
persevering in tribulation,
devoted to prayer,

We stood there lined up against the fence, I don't know about the other boys but I was hoping and praying. It was the first soccer game of the season and the coaches hadn't told us who were the starting players. I had done all I could in practice, running the sprints, doing the exercises, giving all that I had each and every practice leading up to this game. It was out of my hands at this point so I, like the other boys, waited to hear our name read off the list of those who would start the game. It seemed like forever as we waited and then the announcement came, my name was not read off the sheet. I could have given up, spent the time on the bench filled with self - pity but I chose instead to give sitting on the bench all that I had, just like in practice. I still had hope and prayed that next game, my name would be called. About the third game of the season, I heard my name, it was years later when I tried out for my high school team, I made that team and even was named captain and I remember looking back at that first year I played that rejoicing in hope, persevering in tribulation and devoted to prayer had been the difference. So if you find yourself hoping for something, persevere and devote yourself to prayer, it will make the difference!

Peace,
Tom

ISAIAH 40:31

Yet those who wait for the Lord will gain new strength;
They will mount up with wings like eagles,
They will run and not get tired,
They will walk and not become weary.

Frantically we searched, hoping that at every door we opened, every corner we turned, we would find him! The report came in that a small child was still in the house that was on fire. I believe, whether they admit it or not, every fire fighter who enters a burning building looking for a child, prays. The crew I was with searched each and every room we entered, making sure not to leave one thing unturned. With each floor we searched, we never gave up hope, we found strength to go on, searching and not getting tired and then we heard the report on the radio he had been found. As I left the building that day, I remember saying a simple "thank - you" to God that one small life had been spared and thanking Him for the strength to keep going on. Putting our hope in God can have results that bring an inner joy, even when things might not go as we have planned. Hope gives us the strength to carry on so if you're feeling a little desperate, put your hope in God He will give you the strength to carry on!

Peace,
Tom

ROMANS 8:25

But if we hope for what we do not see,
with perseverance we wait eagerly for it.

One of the hardest parts of life is waiting, I mean really who likes to wait in line at the grocery store, or waiting for that package to arrive. I love to fish and the hardest part of fishing is waiting for the fish to bite, sure I can do things to attract the fish, how I jig the line, or what type of bait to use, but in the end, there is always the waiting, waiting for the one moment, when everything seems to come together and you see your bobber go under, or your line reels off or your rod tip bends beneath the weight of a bite but in the meantime we wait, sometimes patiently, sometimes not. When we hope for what we do not see, it can be hard but today's scripture doesn't end there, it goes on to say that with perseverance we wait eagerly for it. You may find yourself waiting and hoping right now for something but the question is are we waiting eagerly with perseverance or are we trying to make it happen ourselves? Sometimes the hoping and waiting is worth it and the fish that takes the bait is a record breaker! In our walk as godly men, we may have to wait eagerly for what the Lord is doing, but we wait in perseverance for His Will to be done.

Peace,
Tom

1 PETER 4:10

As each one has received a special gift,
employ it in serving one another as good stewards
of the manifold grace of God.

It was a simple request; bring what you can to help out the family had suffered a loss due to a recent fire. Their home and belongs were burned so a request went out for help. Men showed up and I was humbled to be one who came to help. I brought my tools, my knowledge but there were others, others who were more skilled in this area and that. Then others came, with food, clothing, and toys for the children. The entire project lasted days and weeks as this family in need began to rebuild their life. As I walked away that final day, when the house was rebuilt and the home rebuilt too, I thought to myself, now this is what church should look like, men and women helping others, helping those in need. I am pretty sure it is what Jesus would have done, if He were still here. That is why its important for us to help like today's scripture shares, to use our gifts to serve one another. The question is are we using our gifts to serve our fellow man.

Peace,
Tom

ACTS 20:35

In everything I showed you that by working hard
in this manner you must help the weak
and remember the words of the Lord Jesus, that He Himself said,
it is more blessed to give than to receive.

It was 3:30 am when the phone rang, it was the medical unit response calling to say that an old neighbor of ours had either fallen or pressed her alarm and needed some help. We had moved to a new home but we were still listed as the first people to be called if Irene needed help, she was a neighbor from the old neighborhood, born in the late 1800. We had built a relationship with her and her husband while we lived next door, Tony had passed away which left Irene all alone in her house, sure there was family but they lived too far away to respond if help was needed - so I got dressed and headed over. She was fine; she had inadvertently pressed her alarm button and was too embarrassed to respond to the medics when they called. I said sure as she asked if I could stay a while, she would put on some tea. That's what today's scripture is truly all about, helping the weak, even at 3 am. Will you answer when the call comes to help?

Peace,
Tom

PROVERBS 19:17

*"One who is gracious to a poor man lends to the Lord,
And He will repay him for his good deed."*

It is the call no one really wants to get, it seems each time we sit down for dinner, the phone rings. On the other end is some type of telemarketer trying to sell this or that, calling for a financial donation or maybe to vote for a certain individual running in the next election, so we decided to start screening our calls, letting the machine get it, calling the 1 - 800 number to take our number off the list. One night we got a call from a local agency that helps disabled Veterans asking for donations of clothing, household items, etc. and I got to think of how that agency, despite helping others, must have to work twice as hard to get donations because of everyone blocking their calls. We do leave bags of clothing out on the porch for them to pick up, there is always something we can give, some clothing no one wears, some way we can bless someone else it is what today's scripture is all about; gracious to a poor man. maybe we need to rethink how we answer the phone, that it just may be God calling… how about you.

Peace,
Tom

PSALM 27:13-14

*[13] I would have despaired unless I had believed that I would
see the goodness of the Lord in the land of the living.
[14] Wait for the Lord; Be strong and let your heart take courage;
Yes, wait for the Lord.*

I never felt the pain of the waiting but I seen it in their eyes.. as a young boy, I was blessed with an athletic ability, so when the teams began to pick sides, I usually went in the first group but there stood the ones wanting to play but seemed to always get picked last.. it may not seem like a big deal as to where you are picked but as a young boy it told you just where you stood in the group.. after a few times of watching the faces of those picked last, I made a promise to myself that if I was ever named captain, I would make my picks a little different.. the despair in waiting can be overwhelming, so we take comfort from today's scripture as we wait.. for an unanswered prayer, a phone call from a loved one, a misdeed to be forgiven.. we find courage as we wait, in the Lord..

Peace,
Tom

2 PETER 3:9

The Lord is not slow about His promise,
as some count slowness, but is patient toward you,
not wishing for any to perish but for all to come to repentance.

OK ready, switch.. we traded positions as we performed CPR on a first aid call we responded to.. the woman had stopped breathing and was in serious trouble as we waited for the paramedics to arrive to take her to the hospital.. with each compression and with each breath, we waited.. it seemed like forever but we continued.. sometimes what we do while we wait can be the difference between life and death.. it doesn't help to count the minutes or seconds as we wait but that we do what needs to be done while we wait.. today's scripture shares that the Lord is not slow about His Promise but sometimes when we pray we want that "instant" answer.. but just maybe He's teaching us patience as we wait.. eventually the paramedics came and so will His Answer - so keep on keeping on as we wait..

Peace,
Tom

PSALM 130:5-6

[5] I wait for the Lord, my soul does wait,
And in His word do I hope.
[6] My soul waits for the Lord
more than the watchmen for the morning;
Indeed, more than the watchmen for the morning.

It was the early morning of my second evening of working nights at the firehouse, when all I could thing about was waiting for the morning shift to come in.. I was assigned the early morning watch at the fire house, meaning I was the man who would receive the call from the Alarm Office if a call came in.. trying to stay alert despite a night of fighting fires, and working the days at my second job, left me weary but being the watchmen meant it was my responsibility to let the others know if a call came in.. Sometimes waiting seems to last forever, trying to stay alert as we wait can almost seem like an impossible job but it is an important one.. today's scripture shares that waiting on the Lord does have help.. we have hope in God's Word, so as we wait, let's hold tight to the Word of God.. it will teach us that the impossible is possible through Him!

Peace,
Tom

PSALM 27:14

Wait for the Lord;
Be strong and let your heart take courage;
Yes, wait for the Lord.

As Carolyn and I waited in the pre - op room for my carpel tunnel surgery that week, we did what came natural to us - but it wasn't always that way.. in life, we will find ourselves waiting.. maybe for a doctor's report, the birth of a child, a long red light, a call from an old friend, a repairman to come fix a broken furnace, a loved one to come to the knowledge of Jesus Christ as Lord and Savior.. whatever the case maybe, we will find ourselves waiting.. so what did Carolyn and I do while we waited.. we prayed! Yep right there in the pre - op room, we weren't embarrassed of our faith so while we waited, we prayed - it brings comfort and peace to those stressful moments.. why not give it a try and like today's scripture shares, be strong and take courage and pray!

Peace,
Tom

HEBREWS 13:16

And do not neglect doing good and sharing,
for with such sacrifices God is pleased.

With all the latest technology, a guy could use a little help.. it's inevitable in today's day and age, that keeping up with the latest computer stuff, email stuff, iPhone stuff and all the other "stuff" out there, that a man my age may just need a little help.. enter one of my daughters, if not all three.. but mostly one of them - she comes to my rescue whenever the "old man" has a computer problem - she may not always want to sit and give her father a lesson on the latest "tech" stuff but she shares the gifts she has been given.. today's verse shares that God is please when we do not neglect in doing good and sharing.. and that goes for her dad as well - thanks Katie for always taking the time to keep me "up" on the latest stuff.. if you have been blessed with a gift or talent, are you sharing it with those in need.. just asking'

Peace,
Tom

2 TIMOTHY 2:2

The things which you have heard from me
in the presence of many witnesses,
entrust these to faithful men
who will be able to teach others also.

Time may pass away but what remains will be our legacy.. I stood for a moment and just looked around - there, gathered together, were men from different churches, different backgrounds, different upbringings, different works of life.. we shared, first a time of fellowship, then a meal, some worship and then heard a message and finally we prayed together.. and I couldn't help but think my good friend Charlie would have smiled.. Charlie went to be with the Lord a year ago, and although I miss him terribly, I know that the gatherings will continue because of his hard work and tireless effort.. today's verse shares about entrusting what we have heard to faithful men who will be able to teach others as well - Charlie did that - he heard the Word, shared it with many men and taught us how to "do men's church" .. it is his legacy and I know in years to come, men will come to know Jesus as he did because he humbled himself enough to serve others - what will be our legacy when we are called home.. will our memory and efforts continue on in others, will we entrust what God has given us to faithful men to continue on.. something to think about.. miss ya' Charlie, say hello to Jesus for me!

Peace,
Tom

GENESIS 8:22

"While the earth remains, seed time and harvest,
and cold and heat, and summer and winter,
and day and night Shall not cease."

The dance of our God - everything has a beat - a rhythm - when we all are "in step" with God and His sheet music - we must sound like a well - tuned orchestra. The problem arises when we, although we play different instruments, try and start a song all to ourselves and keep a different beat than what the Lord has created. Sometimes our music is so loud that it drowns out God's - have we become so loud in our pursuit of our own song that we have missed God's rhythm?   Sometimes after I write these - I look back and see what really am I trying to say - today it's about slowing down and listening for God - to hear His beat or rhythm - it's about submission to God - slowing down - do we believe He is ultimately in charge of all or do we think that our way, our song is better than God's - listen for God's song today - hear the rhythm of His Creation - follow the beat in your own way.

Peace,
Tom

GALATIANS 5:22-23

²² But the fruit of the Spirit is love, joy, peace,
patience, kindness, goodness, faithfulness,
²³ gentleness, self - control;
against such things there is no law.

Have you ever tried to do something for someone and not really give it your all or have enough time so you try to fit it all in - cramming things, trying to do 100 things in the time allotted for 10. The impatience builds until finally things begin to go wrong. Sometimes they go seriously wrong. We, men, are task - orientated people - we watch the clock to see if we can get more done in less time - we miss so many blessings because we fly by them at lightning speed. There is no clock in heaven and all the things God wants to accomplish get done - Amazing. When I walk by my flesh, I find myself trying to do things my way, what I think is best, what I want, I don't take the time to seek God's direction and guidance - I don't walk by the Spirit and it always leads me down the same path - missing the blessings, missing the opportunities to share Christ, His love and the message of salvation. In my confused state, I wonder what kind of witness am I for Christ. How about you, when things get overwhelming, do you walk by the Spirit or the flesh?

Peace,
Tom

PSALM 27:14

Wait for the Lord;
Be strong and let your heart take courage;
Yes, wait for the Lord.

I'll never forget the first time my wife and I drove to Florida - we drove at night and went straight through - about 22 hours. No stopping for anything - I was like a NASCAR driver - our pit stops were to be short and sweet - I look back at the video we took and realized that we had missed an opportunity to share America with our children - they were sleeping and I was more concerned with the final outcome than the journey - is it like that with my walk with God - am I more concerned with just being saved and not the life of sanctification. Well I have learned to slow down and see the blessings on my journey - I have stopped, looked and listened and IT'S AMAZING - the blessings and the opportunity to share Christ are everywhere if we just take the time to slow down and Let God be the director of your life - slow down - take a second or two to look at the life that is passing by so fast - make time to listen to God .

Peace,
Tom

JOHN 10:11

"I am the good shepherd;
the good shepherd lays down His life for the sheep.

"Ut vivant alli" ... I never took Latin in school but when I became a member of the Fire Dept. I learned a little Latin - those words are embroidered in the patch of the Buffalo Fire Dept. - I am sure other departments have them as well - I couldn't just wear the patch without knowing what those words stood for - all the training, rookie school, live burns could only teach me so much but to live those three words meant understanding the meaning behind them - those words mean "that others may live!" - today's verse speaks exactly what Jesus did for us - for all - that others may live - laying down His Life - how far are we willing to go for another - do we just sit Sunday mornings and listen or do we take the Message home and live it so others may live…

Peace,
Tom

ISAIAH 40:31

Yet those who wait for the Lord Will gain new strength;
They will mount up with wings like eagles,
They will run and not get tired,
They will walk and not become weary.

When our lives become all about us and not about Him, we

will inevitably find it hard to wait. Paul often spoke about the trials and sufferings and how they could never compare to the glories that will be revealed to us. (Rms 8:18) But to have the glories revealed we must wait, and wait patiently, secure in the knowledge that God is in control. My wife and I have been in situations where we needed God's hand upon the outcome - we prayed and waited, prayed and waited and trusted, prayed and waited and trusted some more and in His timing - the situation was resolved, but the waiting wore on each of us at different times. I was amazed at how sometimes I would get frustrated waiting and she would have the strength. And then there were times when I would strengthen her - but it always comes down to having faith and trust in our God and knowing He was in control - sure we had the choice to do things our way but I know the outcome would not have been as peaceful and things would definitely be different in regards to the situations we prayed for - oh and what's probably worse is the fact that our relationship with Him would have been tarnished - the trust and faith between God and us would have been broken - I was wondering how long does God have to wait patiently for us to learn to wait on Him?

Peace,
Tom

PSALM 39:6

"Surely every man walks about as a phantom;
Surely they make an uproar for nothing;
He amasses riches and does not know who will gather them.

As I sat down and began to read my Bible and get ready to share - I was in a hurry - I try to get them done by a certain time but I was a little late - so I grabbed my Bible and trying to rush through it, I realized that I was missing the message of each verse I read - then I realized how impatient I was - that it became more about sending them out than reading the Word for myself - I was loosing the message of the message - it became more about getting it out than getting it IN - what became more important - my words or God's Word ? So I humbly repented and sought first His Kingdom and the Message He was trying to tell me - I will try, this day, to be more aware of how much of my time is spent trying to get my goals accomplished instead of His Goals and make the necessary changes - I pray that you too will seek His Truth, seek His Spirit for without it we are lost in a world of us...

Peace,
Tom

ISAIAH 50:10

Who is among you that fears the Lord,
That obeys the voice of His servant,
That walks in darkness and has no light?
Let him trust in the name of the Lord and rely on his God.

Having a rookie on your crew teaches not only the rookie things but those in leadership as well... while working a late night fire, the rookie wanted to do his own thing... I knew that what he wanted was dangerous and would put his life in jeopardy - I had to hold him back and teach him the why it was wrong... When the disciples asked Jesus how to pray, part of His response was that God's Will be done on earth as it is in heaven. For many of us letting go of our will and accepting God's will is difficult - we always think that our way is right and there is a distant second idea that could possibly work but our way is just better for us. Pride hurts our chances of letting God's will be done. There are many reasons we do not let go of our will and let God's will be done - pray with me that our eyes be open to the area in our life that keeps us from letting God's will be done.

Peace,
Tom

PSALM 31:14

But as for me, I trust in You, O Lord,
I say, "You are my God."

We just didn't get there on time... during one of the nights at the firehouse, we responded to a house fire where one of the children had died. I struggled within myself to find the why.... Sometimes it's during the difficult times of testing that we really need to trust in Him and allow His will to be done - it may be painful, there may be tears but do we really think our God who loved us so much to give us His Son would want now to hurt us in some way - He is a God of Love - and He loves each of us despite our shortcomings. I needed to accept that He is my God and learn to trust Him with all the details of my life - the good, the bad, the ugly and most of all during those times when I just don't understand… the question is do we trust only when things go right or do we trust Him in ALL circumstances?

Peace,
Tom

MATTHEW 6

"Your kingdom come.
Your will be done,
On earth as it is in heaven.

While working on a new house job site, I watched the master carpenter … I wanted to be one someday and I was surprised to see him one morning sitting in his truck reading something - I thought maybe the plans for the new house but as I got closer, he was reading a Bible… when I asked him why he said I always ask God for His Guidance for my day - you see we cannot talk about "whose will be done" without mentioning what Jesus told us when the apostles asked Jesus how to pray - most of the time, when we pray, it is really trying to get God to do what we want, or to get us out of a situation - maybe just maybe we are in that situation for a reason - to learn how to trust Him more, or to realize that there are many times when our will is not the best thing but His will is. In fact it should always be His Will - The hard part with that is it means surrendering all of ourselves to Him and His Will and we don't really like giving control of our lives to someone else. Here was a master carpenter being guided by the "Master Carpenter" - so the question is who guides you in the course of your day…

Peace,
Tom

ROMANS 12:6,8

⁶ Since we have gifts that differ according to the grace given to us, each of us is to exercise them accordingly: if prophecy, according to the proportion of his faith;

⁸ "or he who exhorts, in his exhortation; he who gives, with liberality; he who leads, with diligence; he who shows mercy, with cheerfulness."

Has someone who at the moment of our despair has offered us a kind word ever blessed us? Do we remember the feeling that we had inside us? It was, for me, a feeling that someone cared - someone loved me, that my life wasn't that bad - that I could pull out of the situation I was in - these feelings all came because some CARED enough to offer me some encouragement - as today's verses state - each of us have been given gifts, talents, the ability to do certain things well - at no place in the verses does it say "if it fits your schedule " or "if you have the time" or if " it's convenient" or we just wait for someone else to do it - if we profess Christ, we need to do it today - encourage one person today, use the gifts God has blessed you with TODAY - don't wait till tomorrow - we may not get the chance.

Peace,
Tom

COLOSSIANS 2

"that their hearts may be encouraged,
having been knit together in love,
and attaining to all the wealth
that comes from the full assurance of understanding,
resulting in a true knowledge of God's mystery,
that is, Christ Himself,

I often look at people's faces as I am out and about - sadness seems to be full supply - - - their eyes look dull; they seem almost like robots. When you share an encouraging word with them - it's as if a giant light has gone off inside them and they become alive again - from just one simple act of kindness, one simple "hey it will be okay",

89

- - but in order to do that we must step out of our world and into theirs - we will need to be less concerned with ourselves and more concerned with those around us. One kind word can speak volumes to a person - and for those of us who know Christ, it seems to me that it is almost a natural thing to be an encourager - as we walk in the world, Jesus gave each of us an encourager - the Holy Spirit - the helper - I wonder if today we could get out of our comfort zone and walk by the Spirit, and be an encouragement to just one person - just one - if everyone reading this encouraged one person today there could be 100 people who felt a little better today - - the people who were encouraged and those of us who encouraged them - try it - you never know, we could change the world, for Him.

Peace,
Tom

PROVERBS 11

The generous man will be prosperous,
And he who waters will himself be watered.

While waiting to speak at a recent men's event, I happened not notice a man sitting alone, looking sad... I could have just kept busy going over my notes or I could offer a hand in friendship, a word of encouragement...When we start really living for Christ and we become an encourager (looking for those we can encourage), Satan will begin his tricks (lies) - "what are you doing that for? - Why are you wasting your time? Don't you have better things to do? How is that going to help you? What's in it for you?" We can listen to his lies and possibly believe them or we can stand firm in God's Word like today's verse. Not all of us are called to be encouragers, we each have different gifts from God - but if we never tried to be an encourager, we will never know if that's one of the many gifts we have been given - so try it on - see if it fits - each of us can think of one person that could use an encouraging word - all we need now is to step out in faith and think of someone other than ourselves - hey one encouraging word to someone today may help them past the brink of total despair - we could, by one kind word, save a person from making a terrible mistake - wouldn't that be something?

Peace,
Tom

ISAIAH 57:15

"For thus says the high and exalted One
Who lives forever, whose name is Holy,
"I dwell on a high and holy place,
And also with the contrite and lowly of spirit
In order to revive the spirit of the lowly
And to revive the heart of the contrite."

My wife and daughter returned from a four day volleyball tournament - during the four days at home - I saw signs of them living at our house but they were not actually there - I could sort of feel there presence but it just wasn't complete - not until I hugged them late last night did I know that all was well - many times in our lives we feel God's presence but don't feel Him there completely - we have chosen things in our life that have made us more important than Him...Oh sure we keep just enough of "Him" around to feel sort of secure but not 100 % - what are we afraid of - we really need to let go of us and take hold of the concept that He loves us and is there for us - and that His will be done - As the Israelites began there march a crossed the wilderness, God told them He would be with them, never leave them - they had a cloud by day and fire by night of His presence with them and yet they became complainers - finding things they thought God should do for them but they missed all the blessings He gave - are we like that? Complaining of what the God of the universe should do for us - take a moment today and seek out His presence - 100% - submit all of us to Him for He is our God.

Peace,
Tom

JOHN 15:11

These things I have spoken to you
so that My joy may be in you,
and that your joy may be made full.

JOY - what a small word but when we have it - it means so much! Two men were imprisoned but despite what they were going through they had joy - they had so much joy that when the gates of the prison are open and the chains fell off - they stayed there and shared Christ with others - WOW to have that kind of joy in our lives - that despite the circumstances around us - the joy we have in Christ is first and foremost - but so often that's not the case and we fall along the way trying to "get" joy or "buy" joy - joy comes from a knowledge of things greater than ourselves - that we are nothing but sinners and HE chose to love us and send His Only Begotten Son to die for us to have life and life abundantly - you see one day, we will never die - we will live with our heavenly Father for ever and dance on streets that are golden and no more pain or sorrow but joy - and we can have a taste of that today by just letting go and letting God - Paul and Silas let go and let God and when they were freed from prison they chose to stay and share - what would we do if we were freed from a difficult situation in our life - would we stay and share or turn and run.

Peace,
Tom

JOHN 13:35

*By this all men will know that you are My disciples,
if you have love for one another."*

In order for there to be new life, things must die. Nature is the best example of this - as the cold of winter drives us in doors we can still look out windows at the nature around us - if we look to the trees they have all the signs of being dead but deep within them is new life waiting to grow - in order for us to become "new" creatures in Christ - putting off our old self, we must die to self - the thoughts of injustice towards others must die in order for us to live in Him and love all mankind - it is easy to say the words - we love all men but when the rubber meets the road do we - if a person of a different race, social status, or look came to our door and asked to come in for a while because of the cold - would we invite them in? Would we also offer our warmer coat? The reading for today says they will know us by our love - can people point us out in a crowd and say that's one of them - you know, the holy rollers, followers of Christ, those who love... do they?

Peace,
Tom

PSALM 32:8

I will instruct you and teach you
in the way which you should go;
I will counsel you with My eye upon you.

If I ever made lieutenant, I wanted to be just like the officers I had... I remember thinking to myself that if was ever blessed to make the rank of lieutenant in the fire dept., I wanted to be the type of officer I had. Starting a new job can be an uneasy time, starting to run into burning buildings; well that is something altogether different. I realized that my actions as a rookie on the job, could have life and death consequences so I was grateful for the leadership of the officers who took the time to train me - they were the types of men who didn't just say do as I say, not as I do but men who gave 100% to the job! When I think of my relationship with Jesus, He too was the type of leader who lived it. He not only talked the talk but walked the walk. I strive to be that kind of man, although there are moments when my flesh gets in the way, I try to be the type of a man who instructs and teaches in the way Jesus did and I thank God He has His Eye upon me. How about you - what type of a man are you teaching others by your actions or at least trying to be?

Peace,
Tom

2 PETER 1

"for in this way the entrance into the eternal kingdom
of our Lord and Savior Jesus Christ
will be abundantly supplied to you."

Sometimes we can get so caught up in our own life that we forget we have been called, chosen by God to be part of a bigger family - to share eternity in heaven. It is a gift, nothing we can do can get us a ticket there, it was paid for us by Jesus. We can get so wrapped up in our problems and day to day life, trying to fix our spouses, or families or people we work with, or trying to get the next "new" car or big screen TV, that we easily remove any thoughts that this is not the finish line - the old phrase of the guy with the most toys wins is wrong

- someday all the toys we have now will belong to someone else and we will have to answer to God for everything we did or didn't do. Some times my children say to me - "Dad it's always about Jesus with you?" and I respond, "Yes, is there anything else?" When we die and we all will die - what can we take with us but our relationship with our Heavenly Father and His Son and the Holy Spirit - what are we going to do today that will keep in mind that Heaven is the finish line?

Peace,
Tom

1 JOHN 3:18

Little children,
let us not love with word or with tongue,
but in deed and truth.

We may not think of us men as children, but sometimes we need the mind of a child to be open to what God is trying to say to us. Over the years there have been tragedies that can shake our world, tragedies that take loved ones away so I ask you to hug those around you ... those who you call family and friends - realizing how fast all can be taken away - Caring and loving each other is something that we must do better - no longer just lip service but it's time we roll up our sleeves and get to work - but of course it comes down to choice - we can continue to make excuses or we can die to ourselves and gain Christ and love. If we get by the lies and see the truth - we may have a chance - for many years I lied to the fact that I treated my wife and children terribly - the lie was that it was not my fault - it was things that they were doing - hogwash - it was me and the choices I made - it hurt to admit that it was me but through the grace of God, His Love for me, His Spirit of Truth - my blind eyes were open - isn't it time we all take a good look at ourselves and how we care for others - maybe we can stop the next tragedy by reaching out and loving.

Peace,
Tom

1 JOHN 4:12

*No one has seen God at any time;
if we love one another,
God abides in us,
and His love is perfected in us.*

Another community will experience a tragedy…. The sad fact is that it will happen again - somewhere, some time - I wonder about things like - did anyone share Jesus with the young men who will carry out these terrible events - did anyone care enough about them? - I 'll bet each of us can think of one person who is hurting - whether physically or emotionally - I 'll bet that we can think of one child who seems a little distant than the rest - I'll bet that we all know one person who could really use a "hello" today - and we are the ones to do it - but it will take us to come out of our comfort zone - to walk with Christ in boldness - to risk being hurt ourselves so that they may feel better - we can say the word - I care - but do we - are we living for others or is it all about me - We can not do it alone - we need to walk with Christ - He will give us the strength and boldness in His Spirit to love one another - and if possibly we are the one who is hurting - PLEASE - reach out to someone - call a friend - God doesn't want any to perish - there is hope in Him - love each other , care for each other - be open to the Spirit and take the bold step and care for that one who is hurting, even if it is ourselves - God will bless you.

Peace,
Tom

ROMANS 5:8

*But God demonstrates His own love toward us,
in that while we were yet sinners,
Christ died for us.*

There are days when I don't understand His love, but I thank God for it…I guess you could say that there is much to be thankful for if we walk this life with our eyes open… I always thank God for one thing in particular.. it is for my wife. Despite hearing that I had an anger problem, she still married me, and experiencing it in our marriage, she still chose to love me. In dealing with men's ministry I have heard many stories of where a wife has chosen to leave the relationship when things got hard, but not my wife. She has stayed by my side and has comforted me, told me I was wrong, shared with me her intimate feelings and shared the love of God with me and for that I am grateful. That is what I thank God for each day because I know she came from Him…I have rediscovered and each new day discover the huge heart of God. Maybe today, you questioned His Love, life may seem overwhelming but I bet there is one thing you can that God for, we just have to walk with our eyes open, are yours?

Peace,
Tom

ECCLESIASTES 4:10

"For if either of them falls,
the one will lift up his companion.
But woe to the one who falls
when there is not another to lift him up"

So often as I write these daily devotions, I often wonder if anyone reads them and then I get reply from someone who encourages me by saying that they "get something" out of what I write - I always respond that it is not about what I write as much as the Word, the bible verses but it is encouraging to get a reply that says they support what I have been doing. One of the first sermons I was blessed to share was entitled "hey, how ya' doing?" - I shared that a true friend wants to hear the answer to that question and is willing to listen - to share - to encourage and to support and oh yeah one more important thing - to challenge us by asking the hard questions - you know the ones .. hey how you doing with your anger, or with that guy at work who you don't like.. how are you treating your wife and children.. have your read the Word today.. little questions make the difference between a passing person and a true friend.. so I wonder, are we asking the hard questions of those we call friends and better yet, are we asking the hard questions of ourselves.

Peace,
Tom

ISAIAH 41:10

"Do not fear, for I am with you;
do not anxiously look about you, for I am your God.
I will strengthen you, surely I will help you,
surely I will uphold you with My righteous right hand."

When I lost most of my hearing in an accident, I never would have guessed how there would be "blessings amid the pain" - Most of you who know me, have heard the story where an accident at the fire house caused me to lose most of my hearing and you have heard how once getting the hearing aids my life changed. Sure there were the days of struggling with the hearing aids, I had to give up the job with the fire dept., I had to stop building houses, and even my handyman business had to end but as I look back I can see how God's Hand was upon me.. sure there were days and nights when I struggled with it all and even today I still have those days when I have some difficulty hearing but to hear the voice of God through the pain was the best sound I could have ever hoped to hear. I am sure that there will still be days to come when I will struggle with this and that of wearing the aids and trying to hear but the blessings so outweigh the pain. Maybe as you read this you're struggling with some type of pain, physical, emotional or even spiritual but if we do not fear , are not anxious like today's verse shares I am sure we will find all the blessings as we go through the pain and know that HE is right there beside us.

Peace,
Tom

JOHN 5:8

Jesus said to him,
"Get up, pick up your pallet and walk."

I had my driver's license for about 1 year... so when I needed to move my brother's car out of the driveway to get my car out, I didn't think there would be a problem...my mom asked if I would be okay - you see my brother had a manual shift on the column...no problem I said feeling confident... well as I got out and began to drive the car around the block to park it in front of our house, I got to a stop sign and…well couldn't get the car back in forward, I could get reverse but no forward… so I ended up driving the car backwards around the block…sometimes we need to make sure what we are doing before we jump into things…we need to get specific instructions like today's verse shares about getting up and moving forward…I did eventually learn how to drive a stick shift, both forwards and backwards… forwards is much more fun, so let's make sure we know what we're doing or we could just end up going backwards a lot longer than we planned.

Peace,
Tom

PSALM 103:2

*Bless the Lord, O my soul,
and forget none of His benefits;*

Usually when the phone rang at the fire house it meant another fire call or ems call to respond to.. it was early one morning when the department phone rang at the fire house, I happened to be the one to answer it - it was the Alarm Office telling me that we were going to get a visitor later that day.. I ask what it was about and they said "you'll just have to wait and see".. I shared the news with my crew and we waited.. and waited.. and eventually we heard a knock at the door.. standing there was a young boy and his mother, I didn't recognize them at first but as they began to share, it all came back to me.. we had responded to a young boy hit by a car many months ago.. they were here to say "thank you" for what we had done that day.. sometimes it's good to get those types of calls.. you know we don't say "thank you" enough these days and one person who is waiting to hear that is God.. so let our prayer be one where we don't ask for anything but just to say "thank you".. and to those we share life with too..

Peace,
Tom

JOB 8:7

"Though your beginning was insignificant,
Yet your end will increase greatly.

I would never have thought the end would be that great.. many would say that my time on the fire dept. was cut short by the accident that took a majority of my hearing but I say that I was blessed to walk away from the job.. who would have thought that a young guy like myself would find such a love for the job.. at the time of taking the exam to get the job, I had no idea what to expect.. it was a new beginning filled with questions, doubts, even fears that needed to be faced but when all was said and done, the end was increased greatly, like today's scripture shares.. I came away from a job I loved with many great friends and memories, some sad ones too but in the end, I can say my time was blessed.. so if your starting something new, hold tight to today's verse and honor God and your end WILL increase greatly..

Peace,
Tom

PROVERBS 19:11

A man's discretion makes him slow to anger,
and it is His glory to overlook a transgression.

Not until you see it in someone else do it, do you realize how bad it really looks and of course if you had mentioned along the way that you are a Christian, it gets even worse - - - seeing someone lose their cool over things that should not matter...now please I am not saying that we should not get angry over some things going on in life like abortion, child abuse - really any abuse of any kind, divorce, etc. but we must be able to get angry without sinning. I had been with a few Christian brothers when one of them got a phone call that changed his whole demeanor. Whatever was said on the phone caused him to lose his cool... he began to rant and rave, using words that we less than honorable to God, if you know what I mean - as he went "off" I couldn't help but think back to my days of anger... when I too let things get the best of me and my anger - not a pretty sight or memory

I care to remember - today's verse gives us some great advice about being slow to anger and overlooking a transgression... the key is His Glory - are we honoring God when we lose our cool... just asking.

Peace,
Tom

PROVERBS 14:17

A quick-tempered man acts foolishly,
And a man of evil devices is hated.

Most men do not like to get lost and if we are we don't like to admit it... I was lost - while traveling with my wife, we had made a wrong turn somewhere... it was then that I turned to our GPS system and heard the calming voice get us back on track.. I couldn't help but think of the times I was anything but calming in difficult situations.. what was I teaching my children or for that matter those around me in those times of self inflicted difficulty.. I so desperately wanted to be the voice of reason during my times of stress but it never came on my own - only when I heard the calming voice of Jesus - calling me to a peace the world does not know did I find that inner peace in His Arms - you see I finally learned that nothing is too hard for Him.. today's verse tells us about a quick tempered man and a man of evil... we act foolishly and are hated... only in Him can we find that calming voice to get us back on track... the key of course is are we willing to admit we need direction and will we listen to Him...

Peace,
Tom

1 PETER 4:7

The end of all things is near;
therefore, be of sound judgment and sober spirit
for the purpose of prayer.

The alarm goes off, we get up, pray, spend some time in God's Word, get in the shower, do our hair, brush our teeth, put on some deodorant (so we smell nice), get dressed in our best for work, possibly have a little breakfast and head off to work - we think about how our day will be - what we will encounter and how best to handle some of the jobs left over from yesterday .. we think to ourselves that we will do our best to be good workers for we are setting an example of how a Christian man should be at work.. now our day may be a little different but all in all pretty much the same - we give our effort and thought to how we look and what we will do at work but I wonder - do we give the same effort and thought to how we do the most important job we have.. being a family member - whether we are sons and daughters, husbands and wives, parents or guardians, or even grandparents - do we give the same effort to being the best we can be with our family.. the same amount of time making ourselves ready for them .. I wonder if we have ever thought about putting some deodorant on as we come home from work so we smell nice for our families.. now that seems silly but what can we do to make ourselves presentable as we walk through the door to the people we love the most..

Peace,
Tom

1 JOHN 3:17

But whoever has the world's goods,
and sees his brother in need and closes his heart against him,
how does the love of God abide in him?

It never happens intentionally.. we find ourselves busy with our own schedules and "to do" lists, that it keeps us from really seeing the need.. they are out there.. people like you and me, the only difference is they need a little help.. we can find the excuses on why we don't but I wonder if we could ever be intentional about today's scripture and take it to heart about not helping when we have what they may need.. the ending question of today's verse should cause us to take a moment and ask ourselves.. does the love of God really abide in us.. if so, we should act.. a kind word, an open ear, a cup of water in His Name.. those little things can make a difference in a person's life, it will show the love of God.. maybe we will have an opportunity to live God's love by seeing someone in need and lending a hand.. a hand of love.. just saying'

Peace,
Tom

HEBREWS 12:25

See to it that you do not refuse Him who is speaking.
For if those did not escape
when they refused him who warned them on earth,
much less will we escape who turn away
from Him who warns from heaven.

As a house fire burns, it begins to eat up all the oxygen and the thick black smoke begins to bank down until there is total darkness... being only able to see about 2 inches in front of your face, firefighters must find the fire in order to put it out. With nothing to see but black and feeling around as you bump into this piece of furniture and that, groping along the walls, you can get a little turned around and not be able to find the seat of the fire but if you stop moving around, take a moment, stop your breathing - you can "hear" the crackling of the fire - it is only like a whisper - you need to listen close or you won't hear it and if you don't hear it you will go around aimlessly. Sometimes in our life, things can seem to go black - we have lost the "oxygen" to keep going, we seem to be going in circles with no clear direction - it is then that we must stop, take a moment and listen - listen for the whisper of His Voice and once we hear it - we need to follow it or run the risk of going aimlessly in life...today's verse shares about listening... have we heard His Whisper to us...

Peace,
Tom

GALATIANS 5:16

But I say,
walk by the Spirit,
and you will not carry out
the desire of the flesh.

I love the mornings... each morning Dee, our family dog, and I talk a walk - whether it's in the flowery morning of spring, or the heat of a summer morning or the crunchy leaves of fall or in the deep new snow that has fallen through the night - we walk. Why some ask - well for me it is the quietness of those mornings that I can separate the noise of life, of my own thoughts to hear the whispers of God... it's quiet and that means all the distractions of life seem a little less overpowering and I can ask - did God say that? - A time to separate the "my thoughts" from His Words to me - no I don't hear an audible voice but I can feel His Whisper in my heart...and it's nice to take the time to walk with Him before the business of the day comes upon me...and then I end the day in prayer with my wife - a time to let God hear our whispers of prayers and hopes and dreams...when do you take time to hear the whispers of God...

Peace,
Tom

MATTHEW 5:44

But I say to you,
love your enemies
and pray for those who persecute you,

As an officer in the fire dept., you have to deal with men who sometimes tried your patience...whether they disagreed with what you thought was the correct action to take or one that came to work under the influence. When I first made lieutenant, I was assigned to a fire house where one of the men came to work drunk - not falling down drunk but drunk enough to cause problems - most guys would look the other way but I could not - I needed to address the situation the first day I saw it - it obviously caused problems - the man didn't understand why I was "picking" on him - I tried to explain that it was for his own good...each time he showed up for work in that condition, I would call the chief and send him home. During the days, when he came in, not under the influence, I would try to talk with him about his drinking - well over time, he left my crew - I had often prayed for him to come to a place of understanding...well years later at a bible study - who do you think showed up... yep - it was that guy from years before and one of the first things he said to me what " thanks for trying to help me back then - I never forgot what you said to me - I have been sober for over four years now" - those words made me feel glad that I had never turned my head from the problem like so many others - he in fact said that the conversations we had on the good days led him to take a good look at himself and eventually led him to get help...

reconciliation can take many forms in our life and they all deal with a transfusion of hope...where does hope need to be applied in your life...

Peace,
Tom

EPHESIANS 4:2

"with all humility and gentleness, with patience,
showing tolerance for one another in love,"

I remembered when I was a small child - one the way home from school, we used to walk past this five and dime store - there along the counter were jars filled with candy and I remember one time going in with some of the others who were walking home... some purchased things but I was one who gently lifted the lid and grabbed a whole hand full of candy...when I got home, I remember my parents had found the candy and made me go back the next day to return it and pay for what I had taken, I also had to say I was sorry to the owner. I was blessed to have parents who taught me about reconciliation - admitting when we had failed and making it right - the great thing about inviting Jesus in is that we may admit we have sinned but He has made all things right by going to the Cross for each of us - when we come to realize the full nature of the Cross, we are living in the good news of reconciliation.. so I ask - have we been to the Cross lately...

Peace,
Tom

PSALM 133:1

Behold, how good and how pleasant it is for brothers
to dwell together in unity!

Whenever I think of brothers dwelling in unity, Dave comes to mind - a boy who was born with a challenging mental condition - some called him retarded or an idiot but my mom and dad took the time to befriend him in our neighborhood when most turned a blind eye or even worse made fun of him - even today I can be sitting at my parents' house when the phone will ring and it will be Dave - just calling to say hello and maybe talk awhile. That's all he was looking for in life - someone to share in his life - a friendly voice to say hello - most will never know the uniqueness of Dave because of some inner sense that they are somehow better than him…we, who know Jesus, need never to refuse to be quiet in sharing the love of Christ - especially to those who are different than ourselves…come to think of it - we all are different and I bet Jesus never even thought about that as He hung on the Cross for us…so are we living in the good news of unity…are we adding to the separation between men based upon "our feelings" or are we joining together in Christ's unity one to another.

Peace,
Tom

PROVERBS 3:21-22

My son, let them not vanish from your sight;
Keep sound wisdom and discretion,
So they will be life to your soul
And adornment to your neck.

Movies: what am I really watching?". It may seem strange to us adults to have someone tell us what movies we should or should not be watching, and the reality is that we ourselves should hold a standard in our own life as to what is acceptable to watch…I remember the first movie I ever went to see - my grandmother took my brother and I to see Mary Poppins. I remember as she walked us in, got our tickets and sat back to watch the big screen - the movie was so pure and innocent to a child of about five years old, but now I have to say that I haven't been to see a movie in quite awhile - the purity and innocence seems to be gone… there is a standard that I try to hold as I watch any media - can Jesus sit next to me as I watch it…what standard do you hold as you watch…

Peace,
Tom

JOHN 17:15

I do not ask You to take them out of the world,
but to keep them from the evil one.

Okay now be honest... how many of us have passed a sign that said "WET PAINT" and wanted to reach out to see if it is really wet? There's just something about our human nature that makes us want to reach out and touch it - or how about passing an accident... slowing down to see what we can see... way back in the Garden, we all fell away from God when Adam and Eve chose to believe the lie... because of their choice, we, humankind, have within us an evil nature, but the key is whether we want choose to live in that evil nature... there is the old adage that your eyes are the windows to your soul - think about it - we can look into a person's eyes and see if they are having a bad day or a good day...we, ourselves, can choose, by what we see with our eyes, to allow good or bad into our souls...it comes down to choice...what are we allowing into our souls this day...

Peace,
Tom

MATTHEW 5:13

"You are the salt of the earth;
but if the salt has become tasteless,
how can it be made salty again?
It is no longer good for anything,
except to be thrown out and trampled underfoot by men.

I took a moment the other day to look through some of the DVD's that we have here at home. You know the ones your children give you for gifts, ones that we have purchased to watch and I came across a copy of a movie that I would say is my favorite - it is not entertaining but it is enlightening - it is of course a copy of The Passion of The Christ by Mel Gibson. If you have never seen it, I would encourage you to watch it. It truly shows the love of our Heavenly Father and gift of Jesus Christ to each of us. It can be a difficult movie to watch for the scenes are very graphic but it does not hold a candle to what actually happened to Jesus, as He became our sin. If He could do that for us, don't you think we could make sure what we could stand up for Him in what we watch... today's verse shares about being the salt of the earth... have we become tasteless in our living...

Peace,
Tom

PSALM 10:4-5

⁴ The wicked, in the haughtiness of his countenance,
does not seek Him.
All his thoughts are, "There is no God."
⁵ His ways prosper at all times;
Your judgments are on high, out of his sight;
As for all his adversaries,
he snorts at them.

My dad and I would meet sometimes, early before work to cast a line into the Niagara River to see what we could catch and enjoy a moment before work...well one day my dad hooked a musky. As he fought the fish, I could see its enormous size as it jumped this way and that, trying to get off the line. It was one of the largest muskies I had ever seen in my life. As the fish slowly began to give into being caught, my dad began to bring him to a place on the shore where he could land it, when all of a sudden another man, who had been watching alongside us, grabbed his net and reached into the water, hoping to net the fish...in one simple thrust, he hit the fish right where the lure was and in a split second the fish was gone.. a prize fish lost in one moment.. I have to be honest and thought to myself to "how could he do that" "what was he thinking" - I found myself becoming angry and wanted to lash out at the man, snort something like "what are you crazy" but my dad gently reeled in his lure and said "thanks for trying to help" - I was amazed - here I was ready to let loose with a verbal assault upon this man but my dad just gently said - "it happens" and began to cast again. I have learned over the years that fishing with my dad was more than just fishing lessons...they are life lessons that I pray I teach my children as well...what lessons are you teaching as we enjoy God's nature...

Peace,
Tom

PSALM 66:9

Who keeps us in life
And does not allow our feet to slip

We had been fishing for a few hours when we began to notice that the wind was picking up...we had been fishing in a spot where an island had blocked the wind from showing its full force but as we began to turn towards shore to go in for the day, we ran head on into waves and wind that began to beat the boat and cause waves to lift us up and slam us back down. As we continued the trek back to shore, it seemed that each wave we hit was large than the last. We would rise and then fall, as my dad tried to motor us back to safety. It was a ride I will never forget...at one point when I was trying to ask my dad a question that he turned to me and said "pray...just pray"... we were in trouble and it took all his skill and strength and energy to get us back to shore safely. When we got the boat and ourselves safe on shore, we began to talk about what we had just gone through and realized that we had never put our life jackets on...we were blessed to have made in back safe but realized an important lesson...safety first should have been on our minds before we started back to shore. Just like our walk in this life, we can get so caught up in the moment that we forget our safety gear like prayer and reading His Word. Little things that can make all the difference in the storms of life...do you have your safety gear on...

Peace,
Tom

PROVERBS 5:21

For the ways of a man are before the eyes of the Lord,
And He watches all his paths.

Some guys like to hunt or fish alone, but I am one who prefers the company of others as I enjoy the sport of fishing in the great outdoors. Whether it is with a few men like a recent trip or just my dad and I drifting along the current searching for the big ones, there is a sense of fellowship that makes the day seem a little better even if the big one got a way. One time I was blessed to go turkey hunting with a friend. As we walked the fields in the early morning, we felt a sense of peace. Today's verse shares that God watches all our paths, what a blessed thought! Enjoying nature, catching the scent of it, makes me think of what it must have been like walking in the Garden of Eden with God by your side…and the best part of it is, we can experience that today if we are open to His Spirit, if we have a relationship with His Son, if we take the time to get to know our God…have you caught His Scent recently…

Peace,
Tom

PHILIPPIANS 1:10

"…so that you may approve the things that are excellent,
in order to be sincere and blameless until the day of Christ;"

Each species of game or fish have a particular season in which they are allowed to be hunted or fished…there are limits as to how many of a certain kind of fish you can keep for the day…all of these rules and regulations are there for a reason…to keep the fish and game for the next generation and generations to come. Sometimes I have seen a man take more than his limit, going back to the car to dump a bucket of fish and then go back out to get more…it is crossing the line…plain and simple it is wrong. I wonder if we possibly cross the line when it comes to our holiness…do we take advantage of the limits that God has set as His Standards…do we find ourselves saying "well we are only taking them because they are biting now, many times I have been skunked out" - we can always find a reason for doing what's wrong but there is only one reason to do what is right…" Be ye holy, for I am holy" says our God…the question is are we being sincere and blameless until the day of Christ like today's verse shares…

Peace,
Tom

GALATIANS 6:3

*For if anyone thinks he is something
when he is nothing, he deceives himself.*

The other day, Carolyn (my wife) and I were on our way to Sunday service, when we encountered a situation that caused me to see if I was going to live my faith at full throttle...you see there is this man who rides his bike to our church, he is one of the men who directs traffic in the parking lot. It was a cold and wintry morning as we approached him riding down the busy street...I had a choice...I could drive by and "pretend" I didn't see him or I could stop and offer him a ride - offering him a ride meant putting his bike, which was covered in road slush in the back of my new SUV and then having him sit in the seat all covered with the slop that ran up his back...I know what you're thinking...how incredibly selfish...that's what I thought too as I pulled over and said "hey Jim, can we give you a lift?" - living our faith at full throttle means living for others not ourselves - I mean really what did it cost me - a few towels to clean up the truck later in the day to give a ride to another fellow man...almost seems like a no brainer at all if we know Jesus because that's what He would have done or do we think to highly of ourselves and our "stuff"...

Peace,
Tom

LUKE 10:33

*But a Samaritan,
who was on a journey,
came upon him;
and when he saw him,
he felt compassion,*

I just didn't like him... even though we worked together; there was just something about him that rubbed me wrong. He was always causing trouble, adding this and that to an already rough day. I tried to avoid him as much as possible so I didn't let my anger get the best of me... as I left work one day, I walked over to my car and happened to see the hood of a car raised in the air... a usually sign that there was some sort of car trouble - as I began to approach the car, I saw him… it was his car… do I turn around or go over… I walked up and asked him if he needed help and to be honest I was hoping he said NO… he asked if I had jumper cables and could give his car a jump for his battery was dead. He had left his interior lights on during our evening shift… my flesh wanted to say something other than what Jesus would have said… I got my jumper cables and we got the car running… funny thing, ever since that day, things have been better between us - like the Samaritan who helped out in today's scripture, we too have make a difference - the key of course is compassion… thinking more of others than ourselves - so when was the last time you helped out an enemy… it could change their world…and ours too…

Peace,
Tom

LUKE 6:31

Treat others the same way
you want them to treat you.

There were many times as I drove away from home to go to the fire house that I felt bad about leaving them…as a rookie, with not much time on, there were days when I was scheduled to work the holidays. Christmas, or one of my children's birthdays, or an evening at school where they would be receiving an award…there were some nights that I was filled with self pity…why me, why did I have to work this night, everyone should be able to be off for special occasions but this one Christmas night I had to work and responded to a house fire… we managed to get the family out safely and most of their Christmas presents and I thought to myself…that's why I worked as a firefighter… that was a cure for self pity…helping one person, saving a life, making a difference. Living our faith at full throttle is putting ourselves second to the cause of Christ…whether it's our job or picking up a stranger or spending the evening helping a friend - living our faith at full throttle is nothing compared to going to the Cross…so the big question is…do we?

Peace,
Tom

1 JOHN 3:17

*But whoever has the world's goods,
and sees his brother in need
and closes his heart against him,
how does the love of God abide in him?*

My dad and I had just left the dock with his boat as he gave the motor full throttle so we would plane off and begin to go to our favorite fishing spot when all of a sudden the steering knuckle broke and the boat began to circle at full speed throwing both of us to the floor...we managed to get back to our feet and my dad grabbed the controls and slowed the boat down. We ended up fixing the problem but it taught us both a lesson about hanging on a little tighter and not to take things for granted. So here is some simple advice when we are living Faith at Full Throttle, we need to make sure that we are steering in the right direction and hanging on tight to the Steering Wheel (Christ) or we could just end up going in circles...so the question for today is...are we holding tight and pointed in His Direction...

Peace,
Tom

LUKE 9:24

*For whoever wishes to save his life will lose it,
but whoever loses his life for My sake,
he is the one who will save it.*

I am not one you would call an adventurist, I pretty much live a safe life, if there is such a thing...I mean I don't go skydiving or deep sea diving for that matter but on a recent vacation, my daughters talked me into going hang gliding behind a boat...I have to be honest, I was less than thrilled...maybe because I had to take my glasses off and my hearing aids out...and climb aboard this tiny row boat that brought us to a 30 footer where we put harnesses on and then tethered to this long rope and finally strapped to this parachute and as the boat went faster, I went higher...and higher...and higher. Once I got to the height where it stopped climbing and just drifted along, it was one of the most peaceful experiences of my life. I couldn't hear a thing, not because my hearing aids were out but because there was no noise up there to hear and I could see my family pointing and laughing at me hanging there so far above them. When it was all over, it occurred to me that all that fuss about not wanting to go made me feel like I would have missed a great adventure. God is calling YOU to a great adventure with Him…you know He is…you have heard His Voice asking us to climb higher, to live our faith at full throttle and although it may seem a little scary at first, it will be the greatest adventure of your life…so what do you say…let's put the pedal to the metal and live our faith at full throttle…begin the greatest adventure of your life.

Peace,
Tom

1 CORINTHIANS 13:7

"Love…bears all things, believes all things,
hopes all things, endures all things."

When she said those two little words… "I do", I am sure she didn't fully understand what that all meant but I have come to understand that she did! Carolyn agreed in the sight of God and our family and friends to love me for better or worse, and she has, but it has gone deeper than that. She has accepted the better and worse of me throughout our marriage, even on a recent night where she sat home alone as I shared a message with a group of guys. She has loved me through times when I had brought home flowers or the times I had lost my temper, times when we have laughed ourselves to sleep or cried over the days misunderstandings…she has a love that endures no matter what the situations of our marriage have thrown at her and I can only pray my love endures like hers. I am sure there will be many more betters and worse times ahead of us but I know her love endures and I am a better man and have a greater understanding of God's love with her by my side…I pray you have felt that kind of enduring love and love that way too…

Peace,
Tom

EPHESIANS 5:25

Husbands, love your wives,
just as Christ also loved the church
and gave Himself up for her,

I have to get a new one…you see when I sold my old truck, I gave away my bumper sticker that said "I LOVE MY WIFE". I have not had the occasion to get a new one yet but I need to - it was not only a sign to the world that I do love my wife but many times that bumper sticker saved me from leaving her side for a while…you see sometimes when we had disagreements, I would want to run from her - you know get in my truck and drive away but as I approached the old truck I would see the bumper sticker and ask my self - do I? Do I really love her…and inevitably I would answer YES and then turn around to go back and make amends - whether it was to apologize or to understand a little bit better what she was going through, to go back in and fight for us instead of fighting against us…something as simple as a bumper sticker CAN make the difference - what makes the difference for you when things go from better to worse…

Peace,
Tom

EPHESIANS 2:8

For by grace you have been saved through faith;
and that not of yourselves, it is the gift of God;

When we think of better and worse, what usually comes to mind are the times when a husband and wife have come to odds or evens in their relationship to each other but sometimes better or worse can be faced by them together. For Carolyn and I, a "worse" time, was when she had to deliver our stillborn child many years ago. It was a trying time for both of us but I know it was harder for her. To have to deliver a life that she carried within her womb for five months, only to find that precious life had ended a few months earlier, is something I cannot even imagine and yet she comforted me in more ways than she will ever know…she showed courage and love by wanting to see the baby before the nurses took care of this precious life taken so early. As we sat together, seeing this life taken so early, I remember her words… God must have wanted him/her more…in the midst of a "worse" time, she made it better…and for that I am grateful…Jesus did that for us as well - took a "worse" sinner and made us better - oh what Grace abounded from that Cross for you and me…I wonder are we making things "worse" or better…

Peace,
Tom

2 CORINTHIANS 13:14

The grace of the Lord Jesus Christ,
and the love of God,
and the fellowship of the Holy Spirit,
be with you all.

I am sure you have heard that marriage is a 50/50 partnership… well the reality is that marriage is a 100/100% partnership, with each giving a 100% to make it work. Today's verse shares about Jesus Christ, God the Father and the Holy Spirit all working together with us, three in one, working together. There was a time in our marriage when I felt that I was giving more than my share and then there was a time when I knew I was not. Finding the balance of 50/50 was never going to take our marriage to where God wanted it to be, nope - it was going to take 100 percent on my part no matter what percentage she was giving - and vice versa. You see, if we men, are to love our wives as Christ loves the church, then we must be willing to go all the way - like Christ going to the Cross - going all the way, knowing that who He was going for, would fail at times, would miss the mark at times, and would on some days give less than 100%. So I pray, we take a serious look at our marriages, our relationships and really mean I DO for better AND for worse…

Peace,
Tom

LUKE 14:27

Whoever does not carry his own cross
and come after Me
cannot be My disciple.

Today we devote ourselves to "join the revival revolution" and we may think that we will read about some far away country and how the Holy Spirit is moving there but the reality is that today is going to challenge us in ways we never imagined…when I had finally come to grips with losing the fire dept., building houses and my handyman business, I need to ask myself the toughest question I was ever faced to ask…will I live for Jesus or will I live for myself…living for Jesus meant letting go of who I thought I was, letting go of all my desires and to give God the reins of my life…looking back - it was the best decision I ever made but it was hard to die to self, pick up my cross and follow Jesus. That is what Jesus will ask of us today…the question is, will we, pick up our cross and follow Him today…

Peace,
Tom

LUKE 10:2

And He was saying to them,
"The harvest is plentiful,
but the laborers are few;
therefore, beseech the Lord of the harvest
to send out laborers into His harvest.

A few years ago, on the nightly news, four people, two couples who were out sharing the Word, came under attack and were killed on their boat, as pirates overtook their boat. They were missionaries sent by their church to spread the Word of God; you see they were handing out bibles to any and all that were willing to receive them. They could have stayed comfortably in their homes and wished that God's Word was spread to others or they could as they did, join the revolution to share Christ. Each of us are called for a specific purpose under heaven, the question is … will we hide or seek the Truth of where He is calling us to go. I have often been asked to go on a missionary trip, but I always answer the same - God has not called me to go outside the US, there is enough to do right here. I am not hiding for I seek His Direction each day and maybe someday He will call me to cross international lines but for now I have joined the revolution here...where is God calling you...are you hiding from His Call or even seeking it... it may cost you your life, but know this it cost Him His!

Peace,
Tom

2 TIMOTHY 4:2

"preach the word;
be ready in season and out of season;
reprove, rebuke, exhort,
with great patience and instruction."

I remember a few years back, when I first accepted Christ as my Lord and Savior...I was sitting in a bible study and just listening to these guys and girls sharing this scripture and that...I remember feeling as if I was a part of the group but I had nothing to share for although the Bible has been part of my entire life, I never took the time to fully understand what it said. After that meeting, I remember grabbing a hold of my bible and reading with a new passion...I wanted to know what's it all about. How a young boy named David could slew a giant or how a river could suddenly wall up so people could go through on dry land or how a man like you and me could step out of a boat and walk on water...well at least for a few steps anyway. The desire within me grew with each page I turn and although my bookshelves are filled with this book and that, the Bible is my first choice for every verse seems to bring me newness of life or an answer to a longing question. In order to share the Word, we must first learn the Word...so I ask... do you know what's it all about? Are we spending time in God's Word.

Peace,
Tom

ACTS 1:4

Gathering them together,
He commanded them not to leave Jerusalem,
but to wait for what the Father had promised,
"Which," He said, "you heard of from Me;

We had got the crew together and began to go over the plans for the work to be done that day. Each of us needed to be in one accord, working together or else the job would not have been accomplished. Sometimes we had to wait for the materials to arrive but the wait was well worth it, we got to go over the plans for the day and make sure we were all on the same page. Before any kind of revival revolution to occur there must be two things that take place - one is unity for the cause and 2 is a willingness to step outside our comfort zones. Many times as I stand ready to share with men at different men's events, I have this uneasy feeling…a feeling that I would much rather be at home sitting comfortably on the coach, but I am where He has placed me. So too are the many men who have worked behind the scenes to pull off the men's event. We all have a choice - run away or obey and find the power in Him to do what He asks…and each time, as I silently pray to Him for the strength and power, He has NEVER let me down and come to think of it, I come away blessed for doing what He has asked - so I end with one final question…WHAT IS HE CALLING YOU TO DO FOR HIM TODAY - OBEY AND FIND POWER IN HIM.

Peace,
Tom

2 TIMOTHY 2:2

The things which you have heard from me
in the presence of many witnesses,
entrust these to faithful men
who will be able to teach others also.

When the group of men grew to a number where we could no longer meet at the same location, it was time to start another group… each Saturday morning, men would gather at a local coffee shop to share life, we started with five guys but as the group began to grow, we realized that it was no longer beneficial to each other to try and keep us all together. So we decided to start a new group, which meant having to pick new leaders to carry on what we started. We prayed for God to direct us in entrusting men who He wanted to lead the new groups. Today's verse shares about the same thing, entrusting men, faithful men to be able to teach others... so the question is, are we faithful men who would be entrusted to carry on the work of Christ... God calls each of us, to use our gifts and talents and to be faithful... so are we?

Peace,
Tom

1 THESSALONIANS 2:10

You are witnesses,
and so is God,
how devoutly and uprightly and blamelessly
we behaved toward you believers;

As I pulled in my driveway, I saw the dumpster that was parked at Fred's house (my 101 year old neighbor who went to be with the Lord) and it occurred to me that the family was removing all the "stuff" Fred had accumulated over the years...(in 101 years, there is a lot of stuff) and before I entered my home, one of his sons asked me if there was anything of Fred's I wanted...I replied "no, I have the two greatest gifts he could have ever given me...1. The day he accepted Christ as his Lord and Savior and 2. The gift of his friendship, you see for years I had shared Christ with Fred, each time he would say, I am not interested. But one day, 6 months before his death, he asked me to tell him about my friend Jesus. When Jesus commanded us to go and make disciples, He was asking us to do the very thing I hold dear when I think of Fred...friendship and sharing Christ...when all Fred's "stuff" is thrown away, all that will be left is his integrity and memories of his life...when we pass away, it won't be the stuff in our closets and shelves that will be remembered, it will how we lived - I wonder, what will we be remembered for...

Peace,
Tom

2 TIMOTHY 2:15

*Be diligent to present yourself approved to God
as a workman who does not need to be ashamed,
accurately handling the word of truth.*

In all the years of building houses and having a handyman business, I have accumulated a lot of tools…different hammers, saws, wrenches, the list goes on and on and each tool purchased made the jobs I was doing easier. Some of the saws cut wood differently than others, different wrenches to fit this type and that type of use, even hammers to make driving the spikes in or finish nails in place and to be honest since I have left those jobs behind, I have not gone through all the tools I have…maybe someday but for now and the new life God has given me, I find myself using the best "tool" I ever have in living life. That tool is the Bible and for me it has become the Book I enjoy reading and devoting myself to than any other for in it holds the Key to making every job seem a little easier. Today's verse speaks of being diligent, someone who isn't ashamed and accurately handles the Truth. I knew every tool I had when on the job site and how to use them accurately to get the job done. In order to do the job right of sharing Christ, we need to use the right tool and to go and make disciples, we need to use the Bible…so I ask what tool are you using to make disciples - I pray it is His Word, inspired just for you…

Peace,
Tom

1 THESSALONIANS 2:8

*Having so fond an affection for you,
we were well - pleased to impart to you
not only the gospel of God
but also our own lives,
because you had become very dear to us.*

As we took a break, I sat with the young apprentice and began to talk to him. I asked him questions; he asked me questions and we got to know each other a little better. I don't know if you have seen the reports but church attendance has plateaued and in most cases is in serious decline, churches are closing their doors all across America. We have lost those family night dinners around the kitchen table where parents would share their faith over a meal and stress the importance of becoming members of a Christian community and sadly we have no one to blame but ourselves - I think we too often get caught up in the programs that take our attention away from God and on to ourselves - today's verse shares that not only did they share the Gospel, they share their own lives…have we done all we can in going and making disciples, in sharing life with others…are we living God's love by giving all of ourselves as Christ did for us…I wonder…

Peace,
Tom

ROMANS 7:18

For I know that nothing good dwells in me,
that is, in my flesh;
for the willing is present in me,
but the doing of the good is not.

I wanted to get even… I really did! After having altercation after altercation with my neighbor, each time walking away, I wanted to get even, I found myself wanted to get back at him for the way he treated my wife, my family and the verbal assaults that seem to come each time we passed each other… I knew in my heart that it wasn't the right attitude to have and yet time and after time, I felt this way… today's verse shares what Paul thought about his struggle between the Spirit and his flesh… there is a willingness deep inside to do the right thing, the godly thing, and yet our flesh seems to want to take over… after years of this "get even" feeling inside, I decided to pray each time I saw my neighbor, I had to make a conscious effort to seek God, to follow where the Spirit was lead instead of my flesh - sure it's difficult but it can be done in the power of the Holy Spirit… so may I ask, are you praying and following the Spirit or wanting to "get even" by following our flesh… just asking.

Peace,
Tom

ISAIAH 64:6

For all of us have become like one who is unclean,
and all our righteous deeds are like a filthy garment;
and all of us wither like a leaf,
and our iniquities, like the wind, take us away.

As a young boy growing up, I had a terrible habit of lying. Not quite sure why but it always seemed easier to lie than to tell the truth. The only problem was that once you tell a lie, you have to keep telling it over and over and you end up telling other lies to cover up the first one. It was once said that in order to cover up one lie, you must lie seven times and in order to cover up the seven...well you get the idea - before too long you spend all your time trying to cover up the first lie...it eventually leads to a life that is so full of lies that you never remember what you had originally lied about or what the truth really is...a terrible existence, a very bad way to go through life.(maybe that's why I love the Truth so much...) if we go back to the situation that caused us to lie in the first place, we will recognize that we had two reactions to it...one is to lie and the other the truth...there were many times I wish I had told the truth to begin with, so I wouldn't have been so caught up in trying to keep the lie going...coming to Jesus, we are faced with two reactions...1. Lie about our current situation or 2. To be truthful with where we are...one keeps us trapped and the other sets us free...looking back on it now - I wish I would have told the truth more often... how about you - it's never too late to start.

Peace,
Tom

ROMANS 3:23

"for all have sinned and fall short
of the glory of God,"

Recently in using a new program with my computer, I got the message that an error had occurred in how things were going...I had to slowly go back and retrace my steps to see just where I had miss the mark in putting in the correct information. Once I had gone back and found the root of the problem, I could then go ahead and begin installing the new program and after installing the correct information, I had to restart my computer and then and only then would the computer allow me to use the program...we would never think to equate a computer with holiness but if we allow ourselves to think that our walk with Christ is like installing a computer program... making sure we have input the vital info (the Bible) into our lives. If we do not, we need to go back and find the root of the problem (sin) that we may be having (the absence of holiness). Only then will we be allowed to restart our lives and begin to use the program (life with Christ) to the utmost efficiency God had intended for man...so the question is - are we putting the correct information into our lives in order to have a holy solution to our unholy problem...

Peace,
Tom

GENESIS 3:15

And I will put enmity
Between you and the woman,
And between your seed and her seed;
He shall bruise you on the head,
And you shall bruise him on the heel."

I wonder if you have ever encountered this...that no matter what religion someone is, no matter what they may believe as far as their faith is concerned, that when most people, if not all, get in trouble, the first person they cry out for is God...think about it. When things are going bad and they need an escape, they cry out "Oh God help" or if they are about to face a difficult situation they cry out "Oh God help"...maybe even we, during those tests at school when we did not study as we should, we cried out "Oh God help"...or when we made the wrong choice, we cried out "Oh God if you can get me through this ..." or when sickness strikes a family member, "Oh God help", or driving in a blinding snowstorm, "Oh God help" - you see deep down we all cry out for the only cure for chaos...God...our Heavenly Father to watch over us...and He has been there since Adam and Eve started all the chaos by choosing to be disobedient to His Word...so in our disobedience, who do we cry out for...

Peace,
Tom

EPHESIANS 2:4-5

⁴ But God, being rich in mercy,
because of His great love with which He loved us,
⁵ even when we were dead in our transgressions, made us alive
together with Christ (by grace you have been saved),

My older brother and I used to have this toy that was two pieces of plastic shaped in a "u". It looked like human arms and on the end of each arm; there were magnets that were about the strongest magnets I have ever seen. You would put the arms together, to form a circle and then try with all your might to pull them apart. Pull as we did, they would never let go for the strength of the magnets was so much more powerful than the two of us trying to pull them apart. We would, for hours, try to pull them apart but it wasn't until someone else came along and pushed on the right spot that the magnetic force would be broken… you see the magnets reminded me of the sin in our life - always pulling us towards it until we somehow are connected to it - sometimes, no matter how hard we try, we cannot get apart from it…then along comes Jesus, who hits the sin on the right spot and we are freed…like the magnets, we can try and pull ourselves apart but will not be able to unless we find Christ, and like today's verse shares, He will make us alive together… so are you connected to sin or to our Savior?

Peace,
Tom

2 CORINTHIANS 4:5

For we do not preach ourselves but Christ Jesus as Lord,
and ourselves as your bond - servants for Jesus' sake.

As I look back at it now, I think we went too far… Many years ago, I attended a church where on Thursday, Friday and Saturday nights, we would grab our bibles and a crate and go out to street corners and preach the Word. We were told to go "after" the unsaved, those who appeared not to know Jesus. We would stand upon the crates and preach the salvation message using extreme measures. I remember repeating the words 'you are going to hell if you don't accept Jesus!"

Although the statement was true, the delivery was way too harsh to attract anyone to really want to know more about Jesus. I am sure the percentage rate of those who accepted Jesus was considerably lower than if we offered the people some form of help... a little nudge of care and concern as opposed to Bible beating them...I am glad that God allowed me to learn through those experiences to where I have learned to be a nudger not a shover... today's verse teaches about sharing Christ and not ourselves - so are we, sharing Christ or is it all about us ...

Peace,
Tom

PSALM 96:2-3

[2] Sing to the Lord, bless His name;
Proclaim good tidings of His salvation from day to day.
[3] Tell of His glory among the nations,
His wonderful deeds among all the peoples.

OK so here's the problem - we have read the Good Book and it says that anyone who does not know Jesus as Lord and Savior will choose to spend eternity in hell... and we have family and friends who have not accepted the love of Jesus...and we want them to know Jesus before it's too late, so we try to share Jesus anyway we can because we love them but the more we try, the further away we seem to push them...I will never forget my friend who asked me "if I drive out of here today and get hit by a car and die and I do not know Jesus will I go to heaven?" I looked him in the eye and said "NO" as kindly as I could...please understand these are not my rules - I did not write the Book or make the decision to give us the gift of choice - all we can do is pass along the Word of God to those we love - wanting our loved ones to share eternity with God is something we hold dear - but maybe, just maybe we should use today's verse as a starting point, sharing the glories of the Lord, His Wonderful Deeds among the people... are we sharing the love of Christ or the burden of hell - there is a time for each and allowing the Holy Spirit to guide our words is the best way to share...

Peace,
Tom

LUKE 9:62

But Jesus said to him,
"No one, after putting his hand to the plow
and looking back,
is fit for the kingdom of God."

My wife and I took some time to clean some boxes out of the spare bedroom (aka storage room) .. it's a room in our house were we store things that we are not ready to get rid of.. boxes of memories, old clothing that we think one day we will wear again, and odds and ends we have picked up during our 30 years together.. it was okay to go back in time and look at them but it was time to let go and move on so we made some piles.. one for the good will, one for garbage and of course the pile that would go back in, of those things we just weren't ready to get rid of.. I wonder if holding on to them keeps up from moving forward.. today's verse shares about looking back.. maybe it's time to get fit for the kingdom of God and move forward.. what's holding you back, are there things in your "storage room" that needs to be cleaned out..

Peace,
Tom

JOHN 3:5-6

⁵ Jesus answered, "Truly, truly, I say to you,
unless one is born of water and the Spirit
he cannot enter into the kingdom of God.
⁶ That which is born of the flesh is flesh,
and that which is born of the Spirit is spirit.

With a pool in our yard, our daughters learned to swim pretty well. Carolyn and I had taught them many different strokes but when it came to diving, I had to know when to pass the ball to Care's dad, an excellent diver. I wanted the girls how to do a flip off the deck and into the pool but no matter how much I showed them or taught them, they just didn't seem to grasp the concept. It became all about me sharing instead of allowing Care's dad to teach them.. He got the girls on the deck and then told them to hold their ankles and fall into the pool...a

FLIP - wow - something that I had tried over and over, he did with one simple lesson. He had made what I thought was a complicated process seem so simple…where I was trying to shove them in, he simple gave them a nudge. Sometimes when we share Jesus Christ, we need to know when to pass it along to someone else who can simplify the process…some are better at nudging that others and we need to know when it's time to call in an expert nudger who can share Christ…so are we willing to know when to ask for help or is it all about us and our flesh or Christ and the Spirit… knowing the difference will make the difference…

Peace,
Tom

1 CORINTHIANS 9:16

For if I preach the gospel,
I have nothing to boast of,
for I am under compulsion;
for woe is me if I do not preach the gospel.

Get the poles… I love to fish; I even like fishing so much that one of my favorite games with my daughters was "go fish". It doesn't matter whether I am the one catching the fish or the friend who has come along to join me… I just love to fish; I guess you could say that I am compelled to do it. The verse for today shares about preaching the Gospel or sharing Christ, Paul says that woe it is to him if he doesn't share Christ… you see I make the time to fish, I even keep a pole in my car at all times just in case I get the opportunity to cast a line. It is the same way with sharing the Gospel; I love to do it for I feel compelled when I look at what Christ did for me. To be honest, there are a few things better than fishing and taking a man who doesn't know Christ fishing so I can share two of my favorite things…that's if I make the time to do it… we can come up with a thousand excuses for not taking the time to share Christ but only one good reason to share… we were commanded to go and make disciples…what excuse are we using today that will keep us from the only good reason…so what do you say…want to go fishing?

Peace,
Tom

2 CORINTHIANS 5:19

"... namely, that God was in Christ
reconciling the world to Himself,
not counting their trespasses against them,
and He has committed to us the word of reconciliation."

I had the privilege of leading Fred, my 101 year old neighbor to the Lord shortly before his death, but I wonder how many others had influenced his life with little nudges of the Gospel before I came to hear those precious words...Yes I accept Jesus as my Lord and Savior. For 101 years, I am sure many - shared Jesus in little ways along his life but for some reason, Fred never felt the nudge that put him over the edge...come to think of it, I never shoved Fred. What I did was to visit him daily and help him and his 92 year old wife outside on warm days to sit in the sunshine... it was during one of those quiet moments on the bench in front of his house, as we shared the sunshine that the "Sonshine" broke through...all the years of people praying for him, talking with him, sharing the love of Jesus with him led to that day...so never, never, never give up, keep giving little nudges along the way for we will never know when or who will nudge someone to accept Jesus. Today's verse shares how Christ reconciled the world to Himself, not counting their trespasses against them, and neither should we... let us bring a word of reconciliation rather than judgment as we share Christ...

Peace,
Tom

DEUTERONOMY 4:29

But from there you will seek the Lord your God,
and you will find Him if you search for Him
with all your heart and all your soul

I remember the first time I met her...she seemed to sparkle in the light of the campfire. I had been invited to go along on a hayride and that night was the first time I met her. She was wearing cowboy boots, a bluish shirt with jeans on and a sweatshirt tied around her waist...but there was only a certain level of intimacy, for you see she was with a friend of mine…it was years later that I would run into her again…she was working at a convenient store when I stepped in and immediately the feelings I had for her, so long ago, came flooding back. It would be a few months later that the level of our intimacy grew as we began to date and I can honestly say that since that time, each passing day we grow closer and closer because we pray, we talk, we share, we get to know each other and even still today - nothing beats time with her…you see she is my wife and the level of intimacy has grown more than I could ever have imagined. That's how it is with our relationship with God - we meet Him one day and in order for our intimacy to grow, we must have "contact" with Him daily…today's verse says that to find Him we must seek Him with all our heart and our soul…. Even though my wife and I have been married for over 30 years, I still seek her with all my heart and soul, the question is… am I seeking Him with the same… well are we?

Peace,
Tom

1 JOHN 2:3-4

*³ By this we know that we have come to know Him,
if we keep His commandments. The one who says,
⁴"I have come to know Him,"
and does not keep His commandments,
is a liar, and the truth is not in him;*

At rookie school with the fire dept., they taught us about a flash over - where everything in the room becomes heated to the point where the fire flashes over with extreme heat and fire rolls across the ceiling and the temperature in the room climbs very high, very fast, well over 1500 Degrees. We had learned this in the classroom setting and I believed what they told me "could" happen but it wasn't until I went in the smokehouse (a place where training exercises took place), did my experience become more than just belief. You see as we entered the building, our face pieces were covered to simulate extreme smoke conditions and as I crawled to the second floor, the entire building "lit up" with a flash over. The flame and heat was something I hoped I would never experience again. With God, we can have a belief of who He is but until we actually experience Him and His love, our relationship with be nothing more than just belief... today's verse shares that if we know Him we will keep His Commandments...so I ask, have we truly experienced HIM and are we keeping His Commands... for He is more than just a belief...He is God! The great I AM!

Peace,
Tom

MATTHEW 7:21

"Not everyone who says to Me, 'Lord, Lord,' will enter the kingdom of heaven, but he who does the will of My Father who is in heaven will enter.

I have been traveling quite a bit lately and sometimes when I have time to sit and watch the people pass by, I play a little game... I try to figure out what line of work they may be in. Sometimes you can figure it out right away - like when a pilot of an airlines walks by, others seem to be businessmen and women but their exact line of work will take more than a quick look. Just because they may look the part of this or that, doesn't mean they actually are. Some business people dress down for travel, others dress up. It's really hard to try and find out just by looking. Well - being a Christian shouldn't be that way - you know just "looking the part" - there should be some obvious signs that we have spent time at our Savior's feet. Something in the way we live should stand out to the rest of the world...they shouldn't have to ask if we know Jesus... they should be able to say to themselves - "hey they know the King!" - so the question is - what is it that should be in our lives besides looking the part...the sad reality is that today's verse is a very hard one to accept, and yet it is Truth - so don't just call Him Lord, live Him Lord!

Peace,
Tom

MATTHEW 22:37-39

37 And He said to him,
'You shall love the Lord your God with all your heart,
and with all your soul, and with all your mind.'
38 This is the great and foremost commandment.
39 The second is like it,
'You shall love your neighbor as yourself.'

Many years ago, the business world began to share their goals through a vision statement, churches began to write them as well, and then they began to write a mission statement as well. It was a chance to share with the public, what the company or church stands for... what they are trying to achieve as they do "business". I wonder if we as individuals had to write a vision statement, what would they look like... maybe they could be statements like" I am here to be the best husband I can be", "I try to be the best father to my children", "I exist to make a comfortable living and try not to hurt anyone" - some may simply be the goals we set for ourselves on this journey - others maybe little tidbits of who we are, but when all is said and done, our vision/ mission statement should be what we feel is our purpose all summed up in one line. As we read today's reading, we find that Jesus' vision statement was simple "LOVE" - He lived His life to show love, to teach love, to serve love, to be love and maybe we should take part of His life's statement and see if it fits into ours ...if it doesn't, maybe we need to do some serious soul searching about discovering what our vision or mission is in this life...

Peace,
Tom

1 PETER 4:10

As each one has received a special gift,
employ it in serving one another as good stewards
of the manifold grace of God.

I was a junior in high school, doing the usual things guys at that age do, like saving money for a car, working, doing homework, checking out the girls, when one of the teachers pulled me aside and asked if

I would like to be part of a team…immediately I thought of sports… basketball, football - I had played a little of each and maybe even soccer, my love back then but as he continued, he told me about these workers in a city not that far away…men, women and children who were living in broken down houses, some living in old abandoned pickups…he went on to say that they work in the spring of each year planting crops and then in the fall gathering the produce for local farmers…he was not talking about one or two families but groups of families that could only find seasonal worker - they were people of not much education and for the most part they were poor beyond my wildest ideas of poor…so I agreed and began to work on the team that started a campaign to raise awareness along with can goods, financial offerings, clothes, and anything else people would be willing to give to the less fortunate…I discovered that year in school, that life was somehow more important than the car I was saving for or the girl I was trying to get the courage to ask out…finding a cause so much greater than myself…today, we devote ourselves to discovering your serving, about what motivates us beyond ourselves in the Kingdom of God … are we ready to discover life beyond our needs and wants…

Peace,
Tom

HEBREWS 13:2

Do not neglect to show hospitality to strangers,
for by this some have entertained angels
without knowing it.

In responding to first aid calls with the fire department, in the city where I live, we would run into the part of society that no one really ever wants to meet…they were the ones who were down on their life, or some call it skid row, by whatever name we want to use, these men and women, who were urine soaked, filthy dirty and homeless, are children of God - I know it may sound kind of strange to think that these men and women who have fallen on hard times, or have made some wrong decisions, could possibly be children of God but He created human beings in His Image and Likeness and although they may seem very far from being godly, they still deserve to hear the Gospel…but sadly many will turn away and would rather share Jesus with those who seem to "fit" better into our lifestyles...in reaching out and saying Hi neighbor, we need to be able to look past the filthiness and see the goodness in each person...for isn't that what God did for each of us in sending His Son to take our place on the Cross... all need a relationship with Jesus...so the next time we walk by someone who may seem a little down, maybe we could be the one to help them up with Jesus...

Peace,
Tom

PHILIPPIANS 4:6

Be anxious for nothing,
but in everything by prayer
and supplication with thanksgiving
let your requests be made known to God.

Being a firefighter was a weird occupation...what I mean is that most people run out of a burning building but not firefighters. They look at things from a different point of view...when most people see a burning building they think to get out, but firefighters think, "How can I put the fire out!" It is all a matter of perspective but there is a little more to it...firefighters are trained in what to do in an emergency situation - having been through the training, not only fighting fires but first aid situations as well, I have seen the difference when an incident occurs...without training, most people begin to panic, they begin to worry about this and that, some scream, some faint, some become frozen but those who have had the training immediately begin to act...that's how it should be when we get into situations where our faith is tested...if we have done the training, then we can begin to act immediately but of course if we do not do the training (reading His Word, prayer, walking by the Spirit) we can find ourselves in panic mode where we cry out to God to get us out of the situation and possibly God is saying "you need to get through this, it is a testing of your faith...if it is difficult, maybe you need to get more training...and of course do not worry, I am in control"...what tends to make us panic, where do we need a different point of view, what training do we need to complete...

Peace,
Tom

ACTS 16:31-32

[31] They said, "Believe in the Lord Jesus,
and you will be saved, you and your household."
[32] And they spoke the word of the Lord to him
together with all who were in his house.

Sometimes it's the little things that can make a difference... Irene was an older lady who lived next door to us and when she was left alone by the death of a man who lived with her, Carolyn, my wife, and I felt led to stop in day by day just to say hello and see how she was. This went on for years and eventually we moved away, but we remained on her calling list when she would fall or get in trouble and called for help. Although the drive was a little longer, we still felt led to keep in touch and when the call came that she had fallen and couldn't get up, we would go and make sure she was okay and help her to feet. Well years later she died and when the family called to let us know, they said "thanks for making Irene's last few years a little joyful for she looked forward to your visits. Irene's daughter asked as we were about to part ways...why - why did you guys do this for so long and living so far away...the obvious answer was - because that's what Jesus would do...what are we doing today because that's what Jesus would do...

Peace,
Tom

1 CORINTHIANS 9:19,22

[19] For though I am free from all men,
I have made myself a slave to all,
so that I may win more.
[22] To the weak I became weak,
that I might win the weak;
I have become all things to all men,
so that I may by all means save some.

I struggle with doing just that...many of you know I have a neighbor who for whatever reason, is not open to any type of kindness I show. For years I have struggled with just making simple small talk only to find the next day a barrage of foul words and anger directed in our direction. I have tried to mentally write him off but sadly each time I see him, I say to myself that he really needs to know Jesus and yet I can't seem to find a way to crack his hard exterior. I have a great relationship with his son but can't break ground with him. Many nights I have gone to bed praying that God will open his heart to accept the kindness of neighbor but each day it doesn't happen but I will continue to pray for him and gently say Hi and pray that maybe the next time will be the time things begin to go in a better direction. I guess I share this because sometimes when we think in coming to Christ, that things will always come up roses but the reality is that people have the gift of choice...my neighbor chooses his path in life and we must choose ours but we can always have hope that one day, so for now we follow today's verse and become weak knowing in Christ we are strong...what path are you choosing ...

Peace,
Tom

1 TIMOTHY 4:15

Take pains with these things;
be absorbed in them,
so that your progress will be evident to all.

Hey - have we ever seen some one or had to deal with someone who gave the least amount of energy possible to a project? Could we see it on their face that they wanted to be anywhere but here? Have we ourselves been in the same boat - you know only giving a part of ourselves to the task at hand - When I was first married - I was only giving part of myself to my wife - I wanted to be in the relationship when things were good but I had forgotten about the marriage vow that says "good times AND BAD" I was only giving myself during the good times, the laughs, the joys but when it came time for the pain and the tears - I was emotional and sometimes physically gone - and that just isn't right according to God's design - as I began to understand this truth, I began to look at other areas in my life - was I only giving 50% in those areas too?? I began to try and give 100% in everything - that means that I need to see fixing the kitchen sink as a time when I need to give all of me, to do the best job I was able to do - when we mentor or are mentored we need to give the same 100% in giving of ourselves and 100% in receiving what has been shared with us - yes even the criticism - that's the hard part, but with the Holy Spirit with us, we can handle the truth. So how are you handling the Truth about giving more than 50%?

Peace,
Tom

1 PETER 2:5

"you also, as living stones,
are being built up as a spiritual house
for a holy priesthood,
to offer up spiritual sacrifices
acceptable to God through Jesus Christ."

There is no perfect church (well besides the body of believers in Christ - an even now we are not perfect but when He comes again we shall be like Him perfect in every way) Many have said and I would agree - the church we attend has to do with the religion we belong to - knowing Christ is a relationship - which is more important - the relationship with Christ of course- well then why go to church - because we are called to be part of the body of Christ - we should go to exercise that gift given to us - can you imagine the impact on society if everyone first went to church and second those that attended went so to serve others - wow can you imagine where the church families would be - there would be such an awakening by the unbelieving world to want to know more about Christ - in every church there will be conflict, disagreement and even hurt feelings but how we handle them is the real relationship we have with one another - that is where we need to be more Christ like.

Peace,
Tom

PSALM 40:4

How blessed is the man who has made the Lord his trust,
And has not turned to the proud,
nor to those who lapse into falsehood.

Sometimes we can get so caught up in the pursuit of happiness that we miss the blessings along the way…when I was working about 120 hours a week, I thought I was giving my best to my family. Trying to make sure we had enough finances to cover any material thing they needed or wanted. It wasn't until the accident, when I received a little card that simple said "you don't have to be a fire fighter to be our hero", did I begin to understand that work and what it produced was not the gift my family needed. They needed their dad! With God supplying our finances today, I find that I have more time for the little blessings along the way like a quiet walk with one of my daughters, or the hug in the middle of the day, gazing at the stars with my wife, watching the evening sunset, or simple time spent laughing at some funny joke we share. Those "gifts" are from God and are worth so much more than any store bought gift we could ever give... sometimes the best things in life are FREE - satisfying our craving for happiness is finding out that happiness is all around us, if we take the time to actually see the blessings... maybe take some time today and ask yourself the hard question... what makes you happy and how are you going about doing it?

Peace,
Tom

1 CORINTHIANS 13:4-5

⁴ Love is patient, love is kind and is not jealous;
love does not brag and is not arrogant,
⁵ does not act unbecomingly;
it does not seek its own, is not provoked,
does not take into account a wrong suffered,

What's taking you so long… it seemed like every time I was ready to do something on the job site, I had to wait for one of the other guys to help… I found myself getting more and more impatient with each passing minute and day on the job... it got so bad that I was thinking of quitting all together... and then it hit me, when someone asked for my help and had to wait till I finished with what I was going. I had to ask myself, what's the motive of my impatience - most of the time I found myself impatient because I was rushing off to the next thing - today verse starts out with "love is patient" - now it may seem kind of strange to talk about love in the workplace but if we are impatient there, maybe we are impatient with those we love at home. My impatience came because it was all about me... and not about others when it should be all about HIM and if it's not we need to take a serious look at ourselves and our walk with Jesus and what cause us not to love in patience!

Peace,
Tom

PSALM 86:5

For You, Lord, are good,
and ready to forgive,
and abundant in loving kindness
to all who call upon You.

I'm sorry!.. I had said those words so many times while growing up that I began to ask myself if I meant what I was saying. Were they just words I spoke each time I had failed and caused someone pain. Growing up with an anger problem meant that there were times that my actions, words and general attitude did not bring glory to God or even respect to those I lived with. One day while fishing with my dad, I asked him if he believed me when I said I was sorry after I had done a wrong. "Of course I believe you son, and that's why I forgive you for them! was his reply. Today's verse speaks about God's love for us in His Forgiveness and it's not just a simple love but an abundant loving kindness for all who call upon Him. The question becomes that when we say we are sorry, are we really seeking forgiveness or just saying the words to get by... God is ready to forgive us no matter what we have done in our past but we need to be truly repentant, sorry for our actions... are we, really sorry!

Peace,
Tom

PROVERBS 10:23

Doing wickedness is like sport to a fool,
And so is wisdom to a man of understanding.

We thought we could get away with it, but we were sadly mistaken... a group of us kids decided to have a little fun at a local supermarket. They used to pack their old cardboard in the back of tractor trailer on site, so we decided to climb in and have some fun playing around in the cardboard... we knew we were not allowed in their but we never thought we would get caught... that's until one day, the doors on the trailer began to close and we were trapped inside... today's verse speaks about the difference between a fool and a man of wisdom... us kids were fools thinking that we would never get caught, a wise man would have known not to play around in their... so I ask, are our decisions in life, childish and foolish or do we act like wise men of understanding... all comes down to choice! BTW, the driver heard our banging and let us out but not without a stern warning! Maybe God is giving you a stern warning about your choices... just sayin'

Peace,
Tom

PSALM 63:5

My soul is satisfied as with marrow and fatness,
And my mouth offers praises with joyful lips.

There is that old adage that says "absence makes the heart grow fonder" - it has come true for me - you see recently, I was away from home for a few days- all the time I was away, there was a longing deep within me to be near my wife and children (I am so blessed to have a great family) - I had spent the time doing this and that and taking care of some responsibilities that took me away from home. With each passing minute, I became more aware of what I was really missing - I long to be with my family- my wife doing her "things" around the house as I would pass her here and there.. my daughters as they took care of things before another busy week for them - even our dog and cat coming up to me and making me feel "right at home".

Today's verse speaks of God's marrow and fatness, His Blessings and how our soul should be satisfied with it so that our lips will sing praises with joyful lips. When I got home, I couldn't wait to tell them all how much I missed them and loved them. It should be that way in our relationship with God, having this "inner drive" to get back to His Presence and once there, come to realize that in His Presence is love.. so when was the last time you told God you loved Him and sang praises to His Name?

Peace,
Tom

EPHESIANS 3:14-17

[14] For this reason, I bow my knees before the Father,
[15] from whom every family in heaven
and on earth derives its name,
[16] that He would grant you,
according to the riches of His glory,
to be strengthened with power
through His Spirit in the inner man,
[17] so that Christ may dwell in your hearts through faith;
and that you, being rooted and grounded in love,

It was early on in my career as a firefighter, when we were called to Lakefront school for a report of a child not breathing - sure enough when we got there we found a small boy of about 8 years' old who had been hit in the chest by a hockey ball and his heart had stopped, his breathing had stopped .. he was for all practical purposes dead. We immediately began CPR and as the others got the O2 ready, I had started mouth to mouth realizing that every precious second counted.. within a minute, we had the oxygen set up and placed a mask upon his face and continued heart compressions .. and then it happened - He blinked - he began to breath on his own - his heart pumping again - I looked into his eyes and said Ryan you are going to be okay - just keep breathing - we are here for you.. I could sense in his eyes that he knew what I was saying .. his color returned to his face and his eyes never left mine .. soon the ambulance had come and we put him in the stretcher and he was taken away to the hospital .. later I learned that Ryan had a pacemaker and the hit from the hockey ball had stopped his heart and caused the life giving breath to go out of him.. I wish I could say that things turned out okay but sadly they did not.. his weakened body had given out on the way to the hospital and Ryan went home to Jesus but for that one small moment in time I witnessed the power of life and how God must have felt as He breathed life into that lump of dirt called Adam - you see we are all just dirt without the breath of God.. the true Wind Power of our lives.. maybe we should be more grateful and do more with the Breath of Life with in ourselves before it's too late..

Peace,
Tom

EPHESIANS 6:4

Fathers, do not provoke your children to anger,
but bring them up in the discipline
and instruction of the Lord.

"I like it for the beat, the words don't mean anything to me" Statements like this can be heard from children, when it comes to some of the music coming out the industry today - but the sad reality is that the lyrics do mean something - some songs today have a message that is anything but enjoyable. I happened to have the window of my truck opened the other day and a car pulled up.. the boom of the music shook my truck but what was truly amazing was that even with my hearing loss, I could hear the words of the song this young man was listening to.. I cannot even repeat them for they were so vulgar and offensive. I began to think about my daughters and the music they listen to, and how I can apply today's verse in sharing that some of the music today is not God honoring… without causing them to become angry. Maybe just speak the Truth in love and let the Holy Spirit do the work… not a bad place to start! So are we speaking the Truth in love to our children?

Peace,
Tom

JOHN 1:22

Then they said to him,
"Who are you, so that we may give an answer
to those who sent us?
What do you say about yourself?"

Hello - knowing who we are - who we really are can be very frightening to admit to ourselves - what defines us as human beings can be a very sobering thought. We can avoid the whole issue and continue to go about life the same or we can for once in our life, come to grips with who we really are. There are still some days, I spend asking myself what or who am I - I get caught up in letting my job describe who I am - instead of who I am describing what kind of a job I do - In finding out who I really am, I need to have some point of reference - I choose Jesus Christ - the example He set before me is my point of reference - the standard that I try to live by - the example I try to live up to - there are times when I fail miserably but, if I am to be truthful about who I am, I must continue to judge myself against God's Word - some days I fall way short of His Example - those days I cry out to Him " HELP". Although I fail miserably, I would hope that if someone was asked to describe who I was, the first word that would come to mind is - oh yeah Tom - he is a Christian - (only possible with the Spirit's help) - what words would describe you .. .

Peace,
Tom

PSALM 40

How blessed is the man who has made the Lord his trust,
and has not turned to the proud,
nor to those who lapse into falsehood.

Sometimes we can get so caught up in the pursuit of happiness that we miss the blessings along the way...when I was working about 120 hours a week, I thought I was giving my best to my family. Trying to make sure we had enough finances to cover any material thing they needed or wanted. It wasn't until the accident when I received a little card that simple said - "you don't have to be a fire fighter to be our hero" did I begin to understand that work and what it produced was not the gift my family needed. They needed their dad! With God supplying our finances today, I find that I have more time for the little blessings along the way, like a quiet walk with one of my daughters, or the hug in the middle of the day, gazing at the stars with my wife, watching the evening sunset, or simple time spent laughing at some funny jokes we share. Those "gifts" are from God and are worth so much more than any store bought gift I could ever give…sometimes the best things in life are FREE - satisfying our craving for happiness is finding out that happiness is all around us, if we take the time to actually see the blessings…may we take some time today and look with our spirit to see the blessings He has for us today.

Peace,
Tom

PHILIPPIANS 4:9

The things you have learned and received
and heard and seen in me, practice these things,
and the God of peace will be with you.

As we sat around the table, my wife, three daughters, son - in - law, and the two young men dating my other two daughters, it occurred to me that I was passing on something I learned from my father. It was dinnertime and we had all come together to share a meal and before we ate, before anyone took a bite, we bowed our heads to give thanks to God and ask His Blessing upon our meal. We have done this whether we are sitting in our home or out in a restaurant Anytime family gets together is a special day and my dad was on my mind, I realized that I was passing on the tradition, the practice of saying a blessing before we ate because of the example my dad had taught me. It was what I saw him do time and again no matter where we sat to eat, at home, in a restaurant or even grabbing lunch in the boat. I continue because of his example, his lesson to his children to give thanks and as the scripture for today states, there was a peace among us. What example are we teaching, by how we live, something to think about, as those younger eyes are watching and learning!

Peace,
Tom

MATTHEW 11:28 - 30

²⁸ "Come to Me, all who are weary and heavy - laden,
and I will give you rest.
²⁹ Take My yoke upon you and learn from Me,
for I am gentle and humble in heart,
and you will find rest for your souls.
³⁰ For My yoke is easy and My burden is light. "

We don't like to talk about it but we must, in order to understand what happens to our joy...there is a spiritual force that wants nothing to do but rob us of our inner joy and peace that God so desperately wants us to enjoy with Him. That force is called by many names; Satan, the devil, evil...the list could go on and on. The Word says that he even disguises himself as an "angel of light". I know myself that even being busy, thinking I am doing the right thing or God honoring can be part of Satan's plan to rob me of my joy. Someone once sent me an email that said BUSY is "Being Under Satan's Yoke" - I thought that was pretty good, for there are times we can become so caught up in this and that, where we think we are busy doing the Lord's work when in fact we are so busy that we miss the opportunities for joy... you see the devil is a killjoy and wants nothing else but to kill our joy...the question is "WILL WE LET HIM STEAL OUR JOY OF THE LORD?"

Peace,
Tom

ISAIAH 40:26

Lift up your eyes on high
And see who has created these stars,
The One who leads forth their host by number,
He calls them all by name; Because of the greatness
of His might and the strength of His power,
Not one of them is missing.

I wonder if we have ever taken the time to really look at the universe around us. It's not just looking at our planet earth, it is looking at His universe in all HIS glory. Today's reading deals with the stars in the evening sky .. I am always amazed that even though we do not see them during the daylight hours - they are still out there - still shining brightly as if on a dark night where we can see them all - I don't do it as often as I would like but to sit with my wife on a starlit night is truly fascinating - she has studied them and can point out different constellations in the sky - I love to hear her say - look over there that's .. and over there is .. it truly is fascinating but only if we take the time to look - so often in the busyness of our day, we allow the many wonders of God's creation to simple pass without ever taking the time to look .. I wonder what blessings we may be looking past as we go about our daily routines so engrossed with our day that we miss HIS Day! - Take some time to really look at the wonders around and maybe say a "thank you" to our God!

Peace,
Tom

PHILIPPIANS 1:28

"in no way alarmed by your opponents -
which is a sign of destruction for them,
but of salvation for you, and that too, from God."

Our walk with Christ will not win any popularity contests, in fact we may just loose some of our friends along the way - today's verse speaks of being alarmed by our opponents, those who fight against us and speaks of salvation for you from God. These are values we need to keep in mind, but we first have to assume that our values are the ones that match up with God's Word - that we are in fact living the values that we are about to share and that takes a good self - examination as to what we stand for - you know the old saying "people in glass houses.. " Before we get started let's re - examine what we stand for .. is it the Truth that we hold dear to our hearts.. is it more about Him than ourselves .. in the quiet moments of our life, when no one is around to check up on us, are we standing firm upon the Rock of our salvation .. or do we hold the old line of "do as I say not as I do" as the benchmark for our living .. I know tough questions for today but then again nowhere in the Word does it say that following Christ will be an easy road.. it wasn't for Him as He carried the Cross for us .. what are we carrying for Him..

Peace,
Tom

ISAIAH 30:21

²¹ Your ears will hear a word behind you,
"This is the way, walk in it,"
whenever you turn to the right or to the left.

Shhhhh…can you hear it…there it is again…quiet…close your mind to all the sounds of this busy world in which we live and sit there quietly for a moment…can you hear it now…I wonder what you thought at you read the beginning lines for today…did we hear anything as we sat quietly…listening? Maybe some of you thought there was going to be a big bang…or maybe some music to go along with the reading - nope - I wanted us to take a moment and listen - listen for the voice of God in a small whisper. Today's verse speaks of hearing a word behind us… the question is are we listening for it or has His Voice become drowned out by the noise of our world - sometimes we may not hear Him because we never take the time to listen… so tran hear Him - the voice of our Father in heaven whispering to us…I wonder what He is saying to you…

Peace,
Tom

HEBREWS 12:25

See to it that you do not refuse Him who is speaking.
For if those did not escape when they refused
him who warned them on earth,
much less will we escape who turn away from
Him who warns from heaven.

As a house fire burns, it begins to eat up all the oxygen and the thick black smoke begins to bank down until there is total darkness… being only able to see about 2 inches in front of your face, firefighters must find the fire in order to put it out. With nothing to see but black and feeling around as you bump into this piece of furniture and that, groping along the walls, you can get a little turned around and not be able to find the seat of the fire. If you stop moving around, take a moment, stop your breathing - you can "hear" the crackling of the fire - it is only like a whisper - you need to listen close or you won't hear it and if you don't hear it you will go around aimlessly. Today's verse shares about not refusing Him who speaks and warns from Heaven. Sometimes in our life, things can seem to go black - we have lost the "oxygen" to keep going, we seem to be going in circles with no clear direction - it is then that we must stop, take a moment and listen - listen for the whisper of His Voice and once we hear it - we need to follow it or run the risk of going aimlessly in life... are we listening for His Whisper today...

Peace,
Tom

PROVERBS 28:13

He who conceals his transgressions will not prosper,
But he who confesses and forsakes them
will find compassion.

Doing a 180 about sin - wow is that ever true - I remember as a kid going to a miniature golf place - you know where you go around with a golf ball and putter and on the final hole you hit it in and it goes down into a locked box. Well, I had a shiny green ball (green being my favorite color) I didn't hit the ball down the hole - I put it in my pocket - and took it home - I remember feeling pretty good about myself - that I had gotten away with it and no one knew - but I knew what I did was wrong and that seemed to grow on me - the longer I had the ball the worse I felt about it - you see my parents raised me NOT to steal (it is one of the commandments)- I am not sure if my parents remember but when they found out they made me go back and return it - and apologize for it. They may have thought it was a tough thing to do but deep inside I was relieved - I had come clean and acknowledged my sin - and in returning it, the sick feeling in the pit of my stomach was gone. That's how sin is - it feels good at first and then when the reality of it starts to set in - we realize what we did was wrong - we need to own up to our shortcomings, to our sin before we can ever allow God to forgive us - or for others to forgive us - what's causing the "sick feeling" in our stomachs today - we need to own up and come clean and then feel the forgiveness from our God.

Peace,
Tom

ROMANS 15:17

Therefore in Christ Jesus I have found reason for
boasting in things pertaining to God.

I have to admit that there are times when I ask myself "what exactly am I doing this for?" - Whatever "this" is - whether it is helping someone in need, running a bible study, teaching my children a life lesson or even taking some time to enjoy nature - I find myself searching for the answer as to why - and I have come to the conclusion that it should be for the glory of God - you see there was a time when I would do things out of the wrong reason - you know, the times we do things so that others make take notice and say "hey - he's a great guy". I spent many years of my life doing things for "that" reason - trying to please man instead of my God and as I look back I am ashamed at some of the things that I did for the wrong reason - the old saying of " the end justifies the means" should never be attached to the things of our walk with God - our means should justify God or should I say glorify God - in everything we do and if that's not our reason then we should re - examine our "ambition" in doing them - I know - tough message but if we are to be as He was and is - it is the only way to live life .. bringing glory to God. So are we bringing glory to ourselves or to God?

Peace,
Tom

JOHN 17:23

I in them and You in Me,
that they may be perfected in unity,
so that the world may know that You sent Me,
and loved them,
even as You have loved Me.

You know we never get a second chance at a "first impression" - I couldn't help but think of this as I read today's verse and thought to myself that a true first impression is one where we are not hidden behind our pride or self conceit or that we think more highly of ourselves than we should - one area of this is when we need to seek forgiveness - when we have wronged another - it is a humbling experience that can mean so much to our walk with Christ - it takes honesty with in ourselves and within our relationships to admit that we were wrong and that our motives were not following along with those of Christ - that we should love one another - and that we should bless our enemies - but sadly that is not the case of today's world - it has become more about being right no matter what the cost, even if we have to "fake" it. There can be no unity with out honesty and pride will keep us far from being one body, one spirit in Christ. Who would have ever thought that three words together could be so hard to say .. "I am sorry" - is there someone who should hear this from us today?

Peace,
Tom

ISAIAH 52:7

How lovely on the mountains
are the feet of him who brings good news,
Who announces peace and brings good news of happiness,
Who announces salvation, and says to Zion,
"Your God reigns!"

Sometimes we think that life revolves around who we are and what we do. After having to step away from the fire department, due to an injury, I wasn't sure what my next steps would be - it became all about me. What was I going to do with my life? Funny thing, God can turn a disability into ability! Today's verse speaks of those who bring good news, announcing peace, news of happiness. When it becomes all about us, we can forget a simple fact "Our God Reigns!" When we are focused on us, we may just miss the opportunity to announce the salvation of our Lord. When I lost my hearing, I tell people I had to go deaf to hear the call of the Lord! Because of that injury, I share the Gospel! So don't let your disabilities keep you from the ability God is calling you to!

Peace,
Tom

1 PETER 5:3

*"nor yet as lording it over those allotted to your charge,
but proving to be examples to the flock."*

I finally made it… I had taken the lieutenants exam twice and didn't score high enough to get the promotion. It was my third attempt and I did well enough to become a lieutenant in the local fire department. I was flying pretty high as I walked into my new assignment. The only problem was that it became more about the silver bars on my shirt collar than about leading the men. Today's verse speaks about not lording it over those put in our charge but to prove to be an example. I need to get back to being what the promotion was really all about - leading other firefighters by my example not my pride! Is there some pride in our life that needs to be let go of… are we being the examples of Jesus Christ in a way that brings Him Glory, not ourselves… just asking!

Peace,
Tom

DEUTERONOMY 1:31

*"and in the wilderness where you saw
how the Lord your God carried you,
just as a man carries his son,
in all the way which you have walked
until you came to this place."*

I was feeling pretty down. When I had to step away from the fire department, I spent a few weeks in what some might call depression. It was hard getting up in the morning, finding a reason to get up and get started. I just was feeling bad. Today's verse shares about how God carries us and brings us to the place where we are. That may seem kind of strange but despite some of the choices we make, the bad decisions, the turning away, God is still there and willing to carry us until we get better. The first part of the verse is to see how God carried us. I had to begin to look at the blessings I had in my life instead of looking at what I lost. In doing so, I found a reason to get up and get going… God!! Maybe you're down today and need to remember that you are in the loving arms of God... so today, get up for God! Maybe if your up today, there is someone who needs to hear from you that God is carrying them.

Peace,
Tom

1 JOHN 3:18

Little children,
let us not love with word or with tongue,
but in deed and truth.

As I sat last night, with my daughters, they talked to me about this video that was on the news - of how these 8 girls beat another girl up and I mean beat her up badly - the 8 girls along with the two boys who were in on it are in jail and I had to wonder to myself - if they have ever heard of Jesus Christ - I mean what would cause girls to beat each other up and when I asked my daughters - they said that it was all over trash talking.. this is the world we live in today but this is not the world that God made - His World was "good" - - - our sin has made it this way and I have to wonder what exactly are we doing to make it good again.. are we sharing Christ - as individuals, as couples, as church goers, as bible believing people - I am sure we all can sit back and say that we are doing our share - well (and I speak to myself first) we are not doing enough when 8 girls can think that beating another up to the point of knocking her out and then waiting for her to come to so they can do it again - I say we are not doing enough.. join with me in living out today's verse by our deeds and truth!

Peace,
Tom

PROVERBS 13:3

The one who guards his mouth preserves his life;
The one who opens wide his lips comes to ruin.

"You're an...!" The sad reality is that we may find ourselves having uttered something like this. A quick statement filled with anger and hate. The sole purpose was to hurt someone. Today's verse speaks to our mouth; more importantly what comes out of it. When we fire away with our words, someone will get hurt. In the early years of our marriage, I utter some things that were just plain terrible. I would never imagine someone else saying that to my wife but here I was uttering those quick harsh statements. I needed to repent of those and ask my wife for her forgiveness. In meditating about today's verse, I found that I need to do a better job at guarding my mouth and the things that come out of it. I believe, the times when we lash out with our tongues in anger or frustration, is the very thing that can cause ruin in our relationships. The pain that we can cause by a simple outburst of quick spoken words is heart breaking - and the worst thing about it is that those of us who say we know Jesus Christ are setting a very bad witness! So the question is, are we guarding our mouth and the words that we speak…

Peace,
Tom

1 CORINTHIANS 13:5

"does not act unbecomingly;
it does not seek its own,
is not provoked,
does not take into account
a wrong suffered,"

I have not always loved my wife with Jesus in my heart - there were times when it was about me and what she was doing FOR me but when we come to Christ there should be a transformation of ourselves - a newness in our thoughts and actions - we should begin to walk as Jesus walked this earth - with love for each other. Today's verse speaks about such things as not acting unbecomingly, not seeking our own, not provoking, and not taking into account a wrong suffered. In a sense it is speak about living the life Christ shared. In all our relationships, we should be sharing Christ's love and if not it is a great day to re examine what love means to us and how we share that love with those we share life with.

Peace,
Tom

152

ROMANS 6:17

*But thanks be to God
that though you were slaves of sin,
you became obedient from the heart
to that form of teaching
to which you were committed,*

As I entered the building as a rookie fire fighter, I could hear the words of my officer... Entering a burning building seems like a strange thing to do but being committed to the job I was hired for meant changing the way I thought. Before coming on the job, I would never imagined running into a burning building, but here I was. The teaching of those officers from rookie school became so much more than words, it became a way of entering a dangerous situation. Today's verse speaks about a time before we came to know Christ, when we were slaves to sin but thanks be to God that we became obedient from the heart to His Teachings. If I didn't pay close attention to the words taught to me in rookie school, I wouldn't have been much help in putting out the fire. In our walk today, we won't be much help to others if we are still slaves to our sin, what sin do we need to repent from and become committed to the teachings of Christ?

Peace,
Tom

MATTHEW 4:17

*From that time
Jesus began to preach and say,
"Repent, for the kingdom of heaven is at hand."*

As we entered the building, the heat was enough to "make you want to go to heaven instead of hell" but we knew we needed to keep moving forward for the reports were that a lady was trapped inside on the second floor...firefighters hear those words often as they battle the fire within a structure ... "keep moving forward" is the way you find the victim who is trapped or you find the seat of the fire so you can put it out...nothing is worse to a firefighter than hearing the words "back out" - you know that you have not reached the objective and things have gone from bad to worse. That's how it is with our walk with Christ...we need to keep moving forward until we reach the objective... "that none shall perish" - there are no prerequisites in coming to Christ...you don't need to know each verse of the Bible, or how many times Jesus said "love one another" - no we need to come as we are...recognizing that we will fall along the way but even Jesus fell going to the Cross...but He got up and kept moving forward...so if you feel you have fallen...get up and keep moving forward...it's what He showed us to do by His Life's Example...

Peace,
Tom

LUKE 5:32

*"I have not come to call the righteous
but sinners to repentance."*

It always came down to one kid and it always came down to JR. Whenever the kids in the neighborhood got together to play football, or street hockey or baseball, we would pick captains and then they would take turns picking from the group of kids in the neighborhood...of course the fastest, strongest, the ones who could throw the football the farthest or the kid who had a great slap shot would always be picked first and then back and forth, the rest of the "good" players would be picked until there, standing alone, was JR. It wasn't that JR couldn't play or didn't have skills but at some point in the game, he would just kind of lose interest and be "out in his own world". If he was on your team, you would always have to remind him to play defense or it was his turn to bat. Now that I am older and I look back, I can only imagine how JR must have felt each day as he was picked last...I am not sure what ever happened to him...maybe he grew up to be a CEO or lead some great team of doctors or whatever but back when we were kids, it must have hurt to always be picked last. It never occurred to me that maybe JR lost interest in the game because he never really felt part of the team...he was just the guy who was always left last to be picked...I am so glad Jesus never picks us last...in fact each of us are picked first and only...if we were the only ones on the face of the earth, Jesus went to the Cross for us! Think about it...doesn't it make you feel special...to be "part" of His Team now…how are we playing for Him, have we lost interest or are we fighting the fight to win for Him?

Peace,
Tom

PROVERBS 10:32

The lips of the righteous bring forth what is acceptable,
But the mouth of the wicked what is perverted.

"Oh he's just a bum that comes around looking for freebies", "get out of here you bum!" were the words that one of the guys at the firehouse said as Henry came by slowly walking with a limp…You see Henry would stop by the firehouse every now and again and look for a few dollars. We knew that he had spent the money on some type of alcohol and some of the guys seemed a little upset that he would come and ask for money. One night Henry came by and I was on watch…I gave him a few dollars but before I gave him the money I asked if I could ask a few questions…I asked Henry why he walked with a limp…he said he had only one real leg left…I asked if he was always down on his luck…Henry began to tell me that there was a time that things were different but when he came home from Vietnam missing a leg, he never really got his life back on track and now he just drinks… he said he drinks to forget…to forget the pain and each day that goes by, he drinks more to forget the day before. We talked some more, me offering some advice and offering help but Henry just said "no thank you" and asked for the few dollars…I never saw Henry again, I don't know what became of him but I will never forget his face when the one firefighter called him a bum…after all, He put his life on the line for freedom, so let's watch our words and take a moment today and offer our words in the form of a prayer for all those in our military services and their families.

Peace,
Tom

SONG OF SOLOMON 8:7

"Many waters cannot quench love,
Nor will rivers overflow it;
If a man were to give all the riches of his house for love,
It would be utterly despised."

When my daughters were little and we had a birthday party or them, we would play all sorts of games with their friends that came but one game I loved more than the rest...I called it "getting to know..." We would go around the table and see what answers the girlfriends would give when I asked simple little silly questions about our daughters, like...what's their favorite color...or what animal do they love best...and if they could be anything in the world, what would she be...those simple little fun questions built relationships between the girls and their friends. It let the friends know a little bit more about my daughters. It got the girls a little closer to their friends; it was building relationships between them. It was the love of friendship being shared. In our families, we need to be building relationships - and come to think of it - that's exactly what we should be doing with our Heavenly Father too. Little silly questions can bring families closer together, getting us to know certain things about each other that we may just not know and the best part is that it can be fun doing it...today's verse speaks about the man who would give all his riches for love, what we willing to give up for love, maybe the answer to a silly question! ...

Peace,
Tom

ACTS 2:38

Peter said to them,
"Repent, and each of you be baptized
in the name of Jesus Christ for the forgiveness of your sins;
and you will receive the gift of the Holy Spirit.

I left the things that I wanted to do, to go and follow where the Spirit led. There were two separate meetings being held where men gathered, men of different backgrounds, different ethnic heritage. They did have two things in common:

1. Their love of Jesus Christ
2. The meetings had been started by men living out today's verse.

Accepting the invitation to speak at these two events put some pressure on me to make sure I arrived at both events, and on time but the pressure was worth it. In life, we may be called to places and people who need to hear today's verse. Sharing the message might just mean a little extra pressure or hard work on our part but trust me, it will be worth it, to see men giving their lives to Christ and receive forgiveness... there's no price tag on that - what is God calling you to do for Him today?

Peace,
Tom

EPHESIANS 5:1

Therefore be imitators of God,
as beloved children;

A few weeks ago, I spent time driving around NYC and as anyone knows driving there is a challenge. I found myself having people cut in front of me every chance they could...I came to notice the fact, that stuck to my windshield, was my GPS Unit- it was a like a big sign that said "I don't know where I am going, so take full advantage of me" - I found myself caught between wanting to be nice and allowing some to cut in or wanting to tailgate the guy in front of me to keep others from cutting in - I remember thinking to myself, I not being a good witness of Jesus. I came to realize that there couldn't be middle ground when being an imitator of God like today's verse shares. I needed to either let go of the anger I began to feel for the other drivers or pull off the road. In life, things will cause us to take a good hard look at why we do what we do, why we act the way we do... the question becomes, who are we imitating... are we driving in the middle of the road?

Peace,
Tom

2 CORINTHIANS 5:15

"and He died for all,
so that they who live
might no longer live for themselves,
but for Him who died
and rose again on their behalf."

Are we living for what we can get out of life or is there something bigger God has planned for us? For me personally, I will not forget the day I reached out to pull some wires out of an old siren on the fire truck where I worked, and doing so caused my hearing loss. Being that close to it for a short time forced me to walk a new path in life.. I thought for years that I would be a firefighter, house builder, handy man of sorts but God had other plans for my life. I now send out daily devotions, which this book is apart. I never would have dreamed this is what I would be doing but God has a way of making it so we live for others and not ourselves. I wonder what role are we playing in what God is doing on this earth.. where do you fit in? God died for all of us that we might no longer live for ourselves but for Him, so why not start today… living for Him!

Peace,
Tom

MATTHEW 4:19

And He said to them,
"Follow Me, and I will make you fishers of men."

I was reminded the other day, just how much my wife loves me…it wasn't that I took her out to dinner, or that I cooked a meal for her when she got home from work, I didn't buy her flowers or some expensive gift…no I was actually at my worst…sick and as I knelt in the bathroom (not praying well maybe I was) she came and gently rubbed my back, gave me a wet towel to wipe my face and helped me back to bed. Sickness can bring the worst out in us, I have been struggling with a severe sinus infection making me feel just awful and yet in my condition, Carolyn loved me and showed me simple acts of kindness to help me feel better. Jesus does the very same thing as He calls us to come and follow - He says come...sickness and all...just as we are and He wants to show us the Father's love...there are many who will never know the Father unless we share the love of Christ with them just as they are...just as He found us...so maybe we should let the judging be done by someone else and just love them...like we are loved!

Peace,
Tom

LUKE 17:21

"nor will they say,
'Look, here it is!' or, 'There it is!'
For behold,
the kingdom of God is in your midst."

I remember my dad saying to his sons... take the fire exam - it's open to everyone... I remember thinking to myself that I had no prior knowledge of fighting fires except listening to my dad tell us of the fires he had worked and what they did to put the fire out...so there I was, a young 21 year old taking a step in faith to take the fire exam... I was blessed to score well enough on the entrance exam to get the appointment and from there went on to be a lieutenant and retired after 20 years... but what if I never took that first step... what if I let my doubts creep in and actually believed that I wouldn't make it...I guess sometimes we need to take the step of faith and let the outcome be left up to Him. Living for Jesus is more than going to church on Sundays or sitting quietly at home reading your Bible. As important as those are, there is a world waiting for us to take the leap of faith and go where He is leading us and we can come as we are...sinners saved by the Grace of God. Like today's verse shares, the kingdom of God is in your midst, let's go out and grab it by taking the leap of faith!

Peace,
Tom

EPHESIANS 4:31-32

³¹ Let all bitterness and wrath and anger and clamor
and slander be put away from you,
along with all malice.
³² Be kind to one another, tender - hearted,
forgiving each other,
just as God in Christ also has forgiven you.

If I heard those words once, I heard them a thousand times growing up...Tom you are out of control! Growing up with an anger problem meant there were times when I simply was out of control...I said and did things that I am not proud of today but my journey did not stay there...I was told one time by a close friend to let the past of my anger be something that keeps me grounded but not let it be an anchor...(thanks Steve). I spent a lot of wasted years living in the memory of the times I was out of control...it affected my relationships with family and friends and even my wife and children but it wasn't until I stepped back and took a really good look at the times I was out of control and the why...it all came down to one thing...choice! I chose to let my anger and emotions run wild...I was not "in control" - they were and I came to realize that saying "they" were was a poor excuse for not taking control of myself...God showed me that my behavior, when I was out of control was simply...wrong! - I needed to grow up and begin to act in a manner that brought Him glory and honor...and that started with my words...I have to ask myself ...am I speaking in a manner that brings Him glory...what about you...what excuses do you use to let being out of control seem okay...

Peace,
Tom

PROVERBS 18:21

Death and life are in the power of the tongue,
And those who love it will eat its fruit.

I am sure we have all heard the old adage "sticks and stones may break your bones but names will never hurt you" - obviously that was said by someone who has never watched a parent berate a child with adjectives that years later will come to haunt them...I knew this guy who used to tell his child how stupid they were...making fun at every opportunity to poke fun at the childish mistakes that we all seem to make...well years later, when I ran into him, I asked how his child was doing...oh that jerk, he's jobless, still lives in my basement and isn't worth a hill of beans...as we parted I could not help but think that the child grew up just what the father had taught him to be by the words he used as he made fun of him...names will hurt (as I am sure we all have experienced) and those names can kill the dreams of a lifetime of greater expectations. Today's verse shares that death and life are in the power of the tongue...how are our words killing the dreams in someone's life...

Peace,
Tom

MATTHEW 12:34-35

³⁴ You brood of vipers, how can you,
being evil, speak what is good?
For the mouth speaks out of that which fills the heart.
³⁵ The good man brings out of his good treasure what is good;
and the evil man brings out of his evil treasure what is evil.

A buddy and I were discussing how hard it is to witness Christ in the work place when the atmosphere is pretty much a secular thing like a fire house...I am sure you have an idea what it's like to try and share the message of Christ when those around really don't want to hear it. He went on to say that he remembers sharing the fact that he was a Christian, not being overly bold about it but quietly sharing and even reading his Bible during breaks and lunch...he went on to say that no matter how much he shared people just didn't want to hear it. But he remembers the day when he was working on one particular machine and the wrench slipped and he hit his knuckles upon the metal...OUCH! (I am sure we all have done that) well the words that followed were not exactly the best witness and he said that it went through the plant like wild fire...everyone knew within an hour that "the Christian" had swore...today's scripture hit's the nail right on the head (pardon the pun) - what comes out of our mouths is from the heart and the only bible some people may hear is what we utter when things don't go our way… have you slipped recently and wish you could have taken it back…I know I have, maybe we should take more notice of our words, I know others are!

Peace,
Tom

JAMES 3:7-8

[7] *For every species of beasts and birds,*
of reptiles and creatures of the sea,
is tamed and has been tamed by the human race.
[8] *But no one can tame the tongue;*
it is a restless evil and full of deadly poison.

As I write these daily devotions, I carefully read over my words…to make sure that it makes sense and I even used spell checker to be sure that my English teachers won't be shaking their heads saying "I taught him better than that…" - the amazing thing about computers and sending out emails and texts is that you can go over what you say in them before you hit that little button called "send"…if only we had that within our brains before we open our mouths and utter words that can do a lot of damage to those who receive the message…a simple act of thinking before we speak…taking a second or two to rethink of how our words will affect those hearing them can make all the difference… when we speak without thinking, it usually is what we have in our heart…what we have stored up inside us at the moment…sometimes what we have stored up through the difficulties of the day, can come out in a harsh or unloving word….so we must be careful and watch what we store inside during the course of our day…what have you been storing up that could cause harm when it comes out …

Peace,
Tom

ISAIAH 55:9

"For as the heavens are higher than the earth,
So are My ways higher than your ways
And My thoughts than your thoughts.

I sat and thought to myself how do we picture God - is He that grey haired man that we see in the movies - is He just a voice in the sky, is He sitting down right now having a cup of coffee watching us on some big screen TV - whatever or however we picture God, we should come to the understanding that He is not like us in our physical bodies - when we put human characteristics on Him we limit Him to our finite minds and with God that just isn't correct - He is God, the Almighty, ever lasting, the Alpha and the Omega - the list could go one. Today's verse speaks about His Ways and Thoughts are higher than ours. So I wonder if we need to humble ourselves and fear the Lord - not be afraid of Him but fear as in reverence, respect, honor Him - when was the last time we were in awe of Him - it should be everyday - just look around us or better yet look in the mirror -

Peace,
Tom

ISAIAH 66:2

"For My hand made all these things,
Thus all these things came into being," declares the Lord.
"But to this one I will look,
To him who is humble and contrite of spirit,
and who trembles at My word.

I wonder if we have ever taken the time to think about God - I mean really took some time and thought about what God means to us and who God is in our lives - so many people in the world do not even recognize Him and others seem to have forgotten Him. Sometimes we need to - "Be Still and Know that I am God" - so enough said - take a moment today and BE STILL - and know that HE is God.

Peace,
Tom

ISAIAH 45:9

"Woe to the one who quarrels with his Maker -
An earthenware vessel among the vessels of earth!
Will the clay say to the potter, 'What are you doing?'
Or the thing you are making say, 'He has no hands'?

I use to think that I was in charge of my life - setting the time for this and the time for that - working at what I wanted, when I wanted - and I wasn't ever really happy or at peace - there always seemed to be something missing - when I gave Jesus all of me - every part - to live for HIM, I have found a peace - let me rephrase that - He has given me a peace that I could not find anywhere else but in Him. Today people have lost respect for authority; we find ways to cheat the government (render to Caesar what is Caesar's), each other (love one another). We need to come to the place where God is God and we are His humble servants. When I was growing up, I tried to tell my father how to raise me - that didn't go over too big. I needed to realize he was in charge, that's how I learn to respect my boss at work and even my relationship with the Almighty! I wonder, have we ever tried to tell God how to run the world, or what decisions He should make... I think we should let Him do His Thing. Maybe we should step back and watch His Plan unfold today...

Peace,
Tom

ROMANS 3:22-23

[22] *"...even the righteousness of God*
through faith in Jesus Christ
for all those who believe;
for there is no distinction;
[23] *for all have sinned and fall short*
of the glory of God,"

I used to think that if I did everything right, followed all the rules, and tried to please everyone around me- then I would be accepted and get to heaven - sorry to say that most of us know the answer to that type of life - all we get is used and abused and that doesn't get us into heaven! When I came to know Jesus Christ, gave Him Lordship of my life and started to read His Word, I realized that works couldn't get me into heaven. The only thing that makes me "righteous" is the blood of the Lamb. Because of His Love and taking on all my sin, past, present and future - then I could be found worthy of God's Love. Today I try to follow God's rules out of reverence of His awesomeness, out of respect - but I fully realize that I will never be able to repay that debt that Jesus paid for me - but I also am careful not to live in the guilt of my sin - I understand today's readings in Romans 3:23 - that all have sinned - we were all stained with the sin of Adam and Eve - that sin was choosing self over God - it lives in each of us until we believe Jesus Christ as our Lord and Savior and repent of our sin and seek to live a reborn life in Him - if you have not accepted Jesus as your Lord and Savior - please seek Him out today - if you know someone who doesn't know Christ as their Lord share Him with them - you never know - today could be your last chance to do so.

Peace,
Tom

EPHESIANS 4:29

Let no unwholesome word proceed from your mouth,
but only such a word as is good for edification
according to the need of the moment,
so that it will give grace to those who hear.

I wonder if we are aware of what proceeds out of our mouths - any one can just fire away verbal assaults but it takes a prudent, wise person who is filled with the Spirit to keep their mouth shut sometimes - Satan, who is the father of lies, uses everything, he waits like a crouching lion ready to devour our every word against each other but more important against God - he tries to get us to hurt the body of Christ by each of us attacking each other, using joking assaults. I pray that we can become aware of how much damage we can really do - not for ourselves but for the witness of Jesus Christ. The Word says to be imitators of God - some how I can not imagine a conversation between Father and Son and Spirit that turns to put - down humor - so why do we - we need to examine what's behind those "jokingly" hurtful words - last night I had the opportunity to share memories of a movie we all saw - we laughed and laughed - we shared and did not put anyone down and I went away feeling better - does our words cause pain or love, His love.

Peace,
Tom

1 CORINTHIANS 5:10

I did not at all mean with the immoral people of this world,
or with the covetous and swindlers, or with idolaters,
for then you would have to go out of the world.

Often I have heard people say "I want to please God but I don't know what He wants" - come on - we all know what He wants, He wants us to be humble servants, to love Him with all our hearts, minds and souls and strength and to love each other. He wants obedience with our lives - that means when we are in traffic and someone tries to get in front of us we let them in - remember it's not about us - when we are frustrated with our children - that we remember they are gifts from God, when we hear someone is struggling, that we step up and do what God would do - love them. The problem seems that we want to be like the world but as today's verse shares, there are immoral people, covetous, swindlers, and idolaters in the world. I don't think we want to be like them, all the more reason to be like Christ…. So whom do you choose to follow the world or Christ?

Peace,
Tom

PROVERBS 3:31

Do not envy a man of violence
And do not choose any of his ways.

Many don't know this but the original Olympics were designed so that neighboring countries could decide who were the better men rather than going to war! I realize that there is a time to fight but fighting should not be our first option…cooler heads will always prevail but it takes more courage to stand down rather than stand up.

Many times in the fire house, having men in such close proximity to each other, would cause conflicts…when men were exhausted from the days and nights at work, a disagreement would ensue. I have seen the fights and the times when one man would choose to walk away and I was always left with the thought that the man who chose to walk away, was the man who understood that not everything should come down to blows…finding the happy medium between walking away and fighting depends entirely upon how much a man feels he needs to show his strength…it is with much greater inner strength to walk away than to stay and fight…so the question is do we have the inner strength in Him to turn the other cheek in our search for spiritual manhood.

Peace,
Tom

LUKE 6:41

Why do you look at the speck that is in your brother's eye,
but do not notice the log that is in your own eye?

Many times someone has come to me to share a detail of someone else's life…thinking that it was concern for them; they would spill the beans about the details of how this person was off base with an action or comment. If I didn't address it the way they thought, I was sure to get another visit, insisting that I take a stronger position in letting the other individual know that what they did or were doing was in appropriate. I wonder why it is so easy for us to find fault in other's lives but so difficult to see it in our own. I guess, it is the ugly truth of self - deception that makes it easier for us to find fault in another than face the truth of our own shortcomings. I have shared that how I viewed my anger was wrong as I blamed everyone else…and as time went on it became easier to blame others for my own problem. Coming to grips with our own failures and sin is difficult at best but if we hold ourselves to the standard we seem to hold others to, we may just find a few faults of our own that need addressing before we go pointing the finger at someone else. I always say that a good look in the mirror is some of the best home medicine available to us…so why not take some time today and take a good look, I know I will.

Peace,
Tom

PROVERBS 21:2

Every man's way is right in his own eyes,
But the Lord weighs the hearts.

Okay, who hasn't done it…told a little white lie that we thought would never hurt anyone? For years I told myself little lies about my anger. I blamed everyone else, saying that they caused it… when the reality was, that no matter what people did to me, it was up to me in how I reacted. So many times I would justify the anger by saying things like…if they only did this or if they didn't do that, even lies like…I was tired or over worked, or they just didn't understand me. So many false statements on my part made it easier to live with myself. The ultimate lie was "it's not really a problem". Justifying my anger and myself at others expense was the ultimate lie - it made me feel better about something that was wrong. It wasn't until I got alone with G
od and He made me take a good look at myself, did the Truth finally come out. My outrages anger was no one's fault but my own. I needed to stop blaming others and put the blame where it belonged. It was and is MY choice in how I react to the situations around me no matter what others do…I know easier said than done but living for Jesus is dying to self and living for Him. Paul and Silas could have sat in that prison cell and told themselves little white lies about why they were there when the truth was they were living for Jesus…maybe that's' where their joy came from when they decided to sing praise to God, they had a inner peace where the ugly truth of self - deception didn't enter into their lives. We too can have that inner peace, if we don't lie to ourselves.

Peace,
Tom

MICAH 6:8

He has told you, O man, what is good;
And what does the Lord require of you
But to do justice, to love kindness,
And to walk humbly with your God?

In the business world, there has been a trend to make mission statements - clever saying that speak to what the business is trying to accomplish by it's existence - the church has joined in the trend - I have spent many hours with different church boards working on a Mission Statement for the churches .. we have discussed many things but when all is said it comes down to what's God wants for His Church - it is really the mission statement for all those who are believers - it is the core of living each day for HIM and His Will - too often we try to make it about this and that - even making it about ourselves when the bottom line is truly what God wants. Let's get on God's Mission Team and begin to walk humbly with our God ..

Peace,
Tom

REVELATION 3:8

'I know your deeds. Behold,
I have put before you an open door which no one can shut,
because you have a little power,
and have kept My word, and have not denied My name.

With my wife off work and myself getting most of the things I needed to accomplish out of the way, I thought I would have the afternoon to get to some of those things done that I have put off for quite a while but then the phone rang - it was my 100 year old neighbor Fred, who just came home from the hospital after receiving a pace maker.. "Tom", he said "I was wondering if you could run some errands for me, they need to be done right away" Here was an opportunity to live out today's verse. I have to be honest and say that I really did not want to go but Fred doesn't know Jesus as his Savior and being 100, I look for any and every chance to share Christ with him so .. off I went. I didn't share any scripture or even say the name of Jesus but I prayed that my actions spoke louder than any words I could have shared. These little moments in our life, when called upon, may be the best opportunities for giving a glass of water in His Name - let's try and make sure we don't miss them in our effort to please ourselves.. we just may not have another chance.

Peace,
Tom

HEBREWS 5:12-13

12 For though by this time you ought to be teachers,
you have need again for someone to teach you
the elementary principles of the oracles of God,
and you have come to need milk and not solid food.
13 For everyone who partakes only of milk is not accustomed
to the word of righteousness, for he is an infant.

I wonder if as Christians, we find ourselves saying the same things over and over. We need to take a good look at the way we live to see if we are still infants in our walk with Christ. .. To borrow a phrase - "do we walk the walk or just talk the talk". I have to admit that there are times when I wonder if unbelievers could tell if I knew Christ by the way I act - not by my words but my actions - recently my words were called into play and my "Christianity" was questioned - - I have thought long and hard and still continue to have those words haunt me - do I live what Jesus has called me to live - do I love the way Jesus showed me to love.. I can say openly and honestly and ashamedly - not all the time and that is my goal and my sin .. falling short of what Jesus has called me to live - so I pray that you will, as I am, take a long prayerful look at the way we live, at the way we love .. Can others see Jesus in the way we act.. ?

Peace,
Tom

PROVERBS 3:34

Though He scoffs at the scoffers,
Yet He gives grace to the afflicted.

John Wooden, a college basketball coach said, "Sports do not build character. They reveal it!" Many of you might not know this but one of our daughters played volleyball for a local college. She excelled at the sport from the minute she began, in fact as a freshman at her college she made the NCAA second team and as a sophomore she earned NCAA First Team award, but she shocked my world when she announced that she would not be returning to play this year…it was not that her desire to play was gone or that some injury sidelined her, no you see she was standing up for principle and stepped down to show that her coach was unprofessional in the treatment of the ladies on the team. At the end of spring ball, the entire team decided not to return, all for the same reason but as the fall season approached, the ladies went back but not my daughter. She said she needed to stand up for the principle - for her desire to see a change in how the ladies were being coached and treated. She wrote letters to the head of the athletic dept sharing her feelings and informed them of why she was stepping down from the team. She truly showed her character as she was giving up so much to stand up for what was right - she gave up her year as a captain, possibly making the hall of fame someday… she gave up a sport she loved and showed me her true character…as a father watching his daughter play, it made me proud but when she decided not to play, it made me even prouder - I wonder as God looks down upon us as we live our lives…is He proud of what we do or prouder that we stand up for what He has taught us.

Peace,
Tom

1 CHRONICLES 29:12

Both riches and honor come from You,
and You rule over all,
and in Your hand is power and might;
and it lies in Your hand
to make great and to strengthen everyone.

I love to ice fish - I know most people think it's crazy but I joke that it's the closest I can come to be like Jesus (walking on water..) This year I was blessed with a wonderful new fishing shelter - top notch - it keeps the wind and cold out and makes for a wonderful outing on the water (ice). Over the years I have acquired some pretty up to date gear - nice warm gloves, great ice fishing poles and lures - you get the idea I was as modern a fishing guy as many others - well on a recent trip with all my new fancy gear out we went - well we tried this place and that place with out much success - as we were heading out we ran into an old timer named Bill - he had his home made cart and gear and as we passed him we said hello. Since we were not having any fishing biting, I decided to walk over to Bill. When I got to Bill's homemade shelter - a few wooden poles and some fabric - his old wooden tip ups (rods for ice fishing) I found that he was having great success - a bunch of fish laid on the ice - as he sat with his homemade grill, cooking up some potatoes and fish, I noticed he had no fancy gloves, no top of the line boots or lures - just some old basic stuff and it occurred to me that it didn't matter what "stuff" you had but it was the attitude with which he fished - he was an 82 year old man enjoying a wonderful day with the little that he had - maybe our attitudes need a shift from all the fancy stuff we have to an attitude of back to the basics - it's not about us but about HIM and His Will ..

Peace,
Tom

1 CORINTHIANS 10:23

All things are lawful, but not all things are profitable.
All things are lawful, but not all things edify.

Sometimes we are not even aware what the meanings of the

original songs mean .. when my daughters were younger I would sing them to sleep and one of their favorites was "Puff the magic Dragon". Yeah I know - how could you sing a song that spoke of a magical dragon .. and then I heard the stories of how the original lyrics meant smoking a drug. I never bought into those ideas - all I know is that the calming song sung with love would have my daughters asking for "one more time daddy" - when we listen to music and the lyrics, we need to be careful not to read to much into them - it was a child's song that some how has come to mean so much more to different people but to my daughters it will always be remembered as time spent with their dad as they drifted off to sleep. I would not trade those memories for what other people have told me it meant. Today's verse speaks of all things lawful but not all tings are profitable, maybe we need to rethink the reason behind what we do and what brings God glory..

Peace,
Tom

ROMANS 8:15

For you have not received a spirit
of slavery leading to fear again,
but you have received a spirit of adoption
as sons by which we cry out, "Abba! Father!"

At the time of writing this, I know that I am blessed - you see I will be spending time with my earthly father, doing what we both love to do - fish. I try to make time to go with him whenever I can because I realize that one day, he will no longer be with me but when that times comes and for those who were not blessed as I was, to have a father who loves them, nurtured them and was there for them, I can rest in the knowledge that my Heavenly Father has and will always be with men and loves me. Many people in the world point to the many fatherless children as a reason why so many children today find it hard growing up. They have no role model here on earth but if we spend time in the scriptures, we will see a Father's love like no other. God's love for all His Children and me outshines the love of all earthly fathers. There really is no comparison - so let us take a moment, recognize the greatest Fatherly love available to us - our Abba's love.

Peace,
Tom

PSALM 19:1

The heavens are telling of the glory of God;
And their expanse is declaring the work of His hands.

I am not much of what you would call a farmer by any sense of the word but each year I always try and plant a garden. I take the time to prepare the soil, pulling the weeds out, finding rocks and stones while I till the soil, then I lay some fertilizer in and mix it up to be sure that it looks and seems like a good place to lay a seed. I follow the directions carefully on just how deep to place the seed and then cover it up. Then while I water for the next few days, there is a miracle that takes place deep within the soil...from the seed comes the seedling and I am amazed at the tiny seed that begins to grow - I have spent the last few days watching as the seedling begins to take shape and for some silly reason, I think I had something to do with this plant that is now growing, when in reality it is the work of our Creator. So many years ago, HE created life out of nothing but the sound of His Voice and with all that He created He said "it is good"...I must not kid myself and think for one second I really had anything to do with creating this plant life...all I have done is laid some "ground" work for Him to do His Wonder...and if I stop and take the time to think of it... it can leave me dizzy - when have you stopped to look upon all that is around us and give God the glory...

Peace,
Tom

PSALM 104:24

O Lord, how many are Your works!
In wisdom You have made them all;
The earth is full of Your possessions.

I have to admit that I am a bit of a Discovery Channel nut...I especially like to watch the shows where some heavy duty sub goes deep into the oceans...I am always amazed at the creatures that they find miles below the surface - some that have never been seen before - amazing - my daughter Jess and her boyfriend visited a unique farm the other day where they got to get up close to a host of wild animals

- one was a zebra and as I looked at the picture, I commented to her that each zebra has its own set of stripes - no two alike…just like our finger prints, and snowflakes - in fact just like us - although we were all created by God - He has made each of us different and yet we all have His Sacred Fingerprint upon us…what more can I say but to think of the wonder of it all…why not today take a moment and look in the mirror and see God's Creative touch in YOU!

Peace,
Tom

MATTHEW 6:1

"Beware of practicing your righteousness
before men to be noticed by them;
otherwise you have no reward
with your Father who is in heaven.

When we first think of giving, I wonder what comes to mind…I wonder do we ever associate giving with marriage? There was a line from the traditional wedding ceremony that asked "who gives this woman's hand in marriage" - I have thought about the day when I will give my daughters hand over to the love of her life in the ceremony of marriage… when they will give themselves to each other…will they put all agendas aside and join themselves with God, to give all that they have in loving each other? I was blessed to receive the news that a very good friend of mine has asked a woman to join him in life. It was great news for my wife and I have prayed that he would share the wonderful union of marriage. It wasn't that long ago that another friend of mine had done the same and as I thought about marriage and giving, it occurred to me that no greater love does one have than to lay down their life for another and that is exactly what marriage should be - a laying aside all our own personal agendas and coming into a relationship with nothing but LOVE…I cannot help but think of the greatest union we can have in this life and the next and that is having a relationship with Jesus…He has given His all for us… can we say we have done the same? Maybe it's time we lay aside all our agendas and give all we are…

Peace,
Tom

1 THESSALONIANS 5:11

*Therefore encourage one another
and build up one another,
just as you also are doing.*

As most of you know I spend much of my time going from men's meetings to men's meetings and recently I was asked why I spend so much time doing it...I usually joke and say that it is because I live with four women (my wife and three daughters) but beneath the surface it is purely a selfish reason...you see I love to see men, grown men, fathers, single men, husbands, workers of all trades coming together to share the common bond we have - Jesus Christ. I love to see men worship in song and dance (yes there are some men who are comfortable in who they are to dance!) I love to see men fall on their faces before their God recognizing the incredible love He has for them. I mostly like to watch two or three men go and pray for one another - to me it warms my heart and I find the strength to go on and get to experience it once again at the next men's meetings - I really do not have to search for spiritual manhood, I find it at each men's meeting when men gather to praise and worship our God and not be afraid of what the world thinks of them - and to me it is a blessing - I pray that the men who are reading this will find a group of men to experience what I do, and if you cannot find one - start one - or call me and we will start one together.

Peace,
Tom

PSALM 38:15

*For I hope in You, O Lord;
You will answer, O Lord my God.*

I was speaking to a gentleman the other day, which happens to read my daily messages. He made a comment to me that made me stop the conversation to address what he said, if I could be half the man you are, how do you do it? When I asked him what he meant, he asked what's your secret, how do you live such a godly life? Well first off I said, I recognize that I am a sinner saved by the grace of

God, nothing I did, do or will do will ever repay the debt that Jesus Christ paid for with His Life, secondly I pray. Today's verse is a line from an old hymn and I find strength for today and bright hope for tomorrow. Strength for today, cause I know I need Him every step, hope for tomorrow, because I know I need that even more. There is no secret, I am an ordinary man who falls to temptation, says the wrong things at times, makes mistakes along the way and the biggest thing I try to remember is that it's not about me, but about Him. I am humbled that he would think I live a godly life, for I know I fall at times but try to make each moment count! No secret, it is what Jesus did and to be a follower of His, it is what we must do! So, don't ever hope to be like me, hope and live to be like HIM!

Peace,
Tom

PHILIPPIANS 4:12

I know how to get along with humble means,
and I also know how to live in prosperity;
in any and every circumstance
I have learned the secret of being filled and going hungry,
both of having abundance and suffering need.

I don't know if you heard this one but it is making its way around… "Don't tell God how big the mountain is, tell the mountain how big your God is" - recently while driving through West Virginia, I thought to myself, how does he do it…I was speaking to myself about a pastor friend of mine who rides his bike home from Buffalo NY to visit his family…I thought to myself as I drove up each mountain…I can't believe he can bike these - it seemed as if each mountain got bigger and bigger, steeper and steeper but then it occurred to me that once you reach the top…it's all downhill from there - at the top of every mountain is a course correction - you don't need to peddle as hard, in fact you don't even need to peddle at all but the key is peddling as hard as you can as you climb higher and higher and the closer you get to the top, the harder it is…dropping the weight of worry, as we face the mountains in our life, means working hard as we get closer to the pinnacle - as we move closer to God, we will have to work harder and rely on Him more…but there is the downside of the mountain coming…just hang on to Him and then we can enjoy the ride…I pray that we have lightened our load when it comes to worry, that we learn a little about letting go…now it's time to put what we learned into action and I am not worried at all that we will…if we work hard and trust Him more.

Peace,
Tom

2 CORINTHIANS 8:7

But just as you abound in everything,
in faith and utterance and knowledge and in all earnestness
and in the love we inspired in you,
see that you abound in this gracious work also.

My father in law was a man of few words; he was a callous man, not in attitude but in life itself. He was a hard workingman, a carpenter and someone who could take an old dingy bathroom or kitchen and turn it into a beautiful new room. He could also build things like houses, garages, cabinets and many others. He could do tile work, concrete, rough carpentry and finished work as well. He worked very hard all his life and his body showed it. He has since gone to be with the Lord but our house is filled with him in the many gifts he gave us…like a bathroom vanity made from scratch, or the cabinet our television sits on and there are others all around our house - Carolyn and I have a feel that his spirit lives on in the many works of his hands but the greatest gift he gave to me was his daughter. I still remember the day I asked for her hand in marriage and his words to me were.. "Take care of her, do the little things that make life happy, keep a good roof over her head and love her" - those were great words that I have never forgotten. I have tried to live those words, failing sometimes here and there but I have come to realize that in living the giving life, it is the little things that make the difference and many of the things we give will live on long after we have left this world…so I ask, what are we giving that will live on after we leave this earthly place…

Peace,
Tom

2 CORINTHIANS 8:2

*"that in a great ordeal of affliction their abundance of joy
and their deep poverty overflowed
in the wealth of their liberality."*

Sometimes it's not how much we give, but it is the way in which we give that makes the difference. I am blessed to have grown up in a family where my mom and dad taught me the gift of giving and giving generously. Many times when we would be driving along and we would come to a toll, my dad would pay for the next person in line. Not that it was anything great but it was just something to brighten someone's day. There were also the times when we would be at a restaurant and my dad would pick up the bill for some family sharing a meal, just to pass along the blessings that he received in the form of a great job and a good wage. It's the small things that can turn a person's day around and make them realize that life is full of surprises. Like that unexpected call from a friend just to say hello, or the card in the mail that says "hey I was thinking of you". There are hundreds if not thousands of opportunities to live the giving life, if we just take the time to be aware of them. Even something as small as opening a door to a store, can make a person feel special. So what do you say...shall we do small things, all in the name of love?

Peace,
Tom

MATTHEW 16:24

*Then Jesus said to His disciples,
"If anyone wishes to come after Me, he must deny himself,
and take up his cross and follow Me.*

One Christmas, Becky, our youngest daughter, and myself brought home a unwanted gift from our Christmas celebration with family...we brought with us the "flu" bug that was going around. I had to laugh because it seemed as if Becky was "following her father" as we each spent time in the bathroom. The amazing thing is that through the sickness, I got to see a timeless insight on God's guidance...dying to self - you see my wife gave of her day to take care of Becky and me…getting us ice chips, crackers, a simple rub on the shoulder in helping us feel a little better. She worked tirelessly as she cared for each of us in a way that made us feel special on a day when we felt… well really bad. Watching someone show love, despite how they feel about it (I am sure Carolyn did not want to spend her day that way) is just what Jesus did by going to the Cross - He saw the Fathers love for His Children and gave His Life so we would know the Father's love…I wonder - how are we denying ourselves, taking up His Cross and following Him to show God's love…

Peace,
Tom

1 CORINTHIANS 11:2

Now I praise you
because you remember me in everything
and hold firmly to the traditions,
just as I delivered them to you.

Sometimes late at night, when I had the early morning watch at the fire house, I would look back at all the "journals" we kept…the journals were the records of all the calls our company had gone on… some dated back many years…I would go through them and see all the fire calls, ems calls we had responded to, remembering this call and that, how this fire went out fast, how we rescued someone from that one…and I got to thinking about how important it is to remember past prayers as well…prayers that were answered the way we wanted them to be answered and prayers that were answered the way He thought best. An old pastor once told me to keep a prayer journal, this way you could look back and see how God answered prayer…and I got to thinking about the very first prayer I remember…it was by the side of my bed as my parents knelt to say our evening prayers.. maybe you remember it too… "Now I lay me down to sleep, I pray the Lord my soul to keep…" I wonder if other parents are still praying that prayer with their children today…in either case, I hope your praying…and even keeping a journal of how much God loves you…

Peace,
Tom

ISAIAH 43:18

"Do not call to mind the former things,
Or ponder things of the past.

When my dad and I go fishing, we usually drift along but sometimes when the wind is strong, we throw out an anchor...well this particular day, we had to throw out two...one on the front of the boat and one out the back...we spent the day catching fish and when evening came, it was time to go so we pulled up the anchor and started up the motor...as we began to rev the motor, we noticed that we weren't moving...immediately we thought something was wrong with the propeller but as we went back to look, we noticed the rear anchor line...it was the anchor that was holding us back from moving forward...sure anchors are good when things get rough but sometimes in life, we can allow our past to be our anchors...keeping us from moving forward, not letting go of the things that we can do nothing about...today's scripture shares a great point about letting go of former things and not pondering on the past...so let's let go of the anchors that are holding us back and begin to move forward...otherwise we stay in the same spot as yesterday...

Peace,
Tom

PROVERBS 4:25

Let your eyes look directly ahead
And let your gaze be fixed straight in front of you.

With one roll of the dice, I found myself falling way back in the game.. no I wasn't gambling.. I was playing a game of "chutes and ladders", maybe you remember it. It was a childhood game where you moved your pawn piece across the board depending on the number of spots on the dice.. if you landed on a space with a ladder, you climbed to a higher level but if you landed on a chute, you went back spaces.. sometimes in life, we can feel like we are rolling the dice on the decisions we need to make.. they may take us up or down depending on how we decide.. today's verse tells us where to keep our eyes and our gaze as we go through the game of life.. another great childhood game as well.. so let's keep our focus straight ahead.. or we may just find ourselves backing up a few spaces..

Peace,
Tom

MATTHEW 5:42

Give to him who asks of you,
and do not turn away from him
who wants to borrow from you.

When I was a younger man, I got caught up in the "my stuff" attitude.. when I started working and learning what it took to make a dollar, I began to worry about "my stuff".. not so much when I used it but when someone asked to borrow something of "mine".. I remember many times fighting within myself to either share what I had or keep it for myself.. I had lent some things out in the past and they usually came back a little broken or not as I kept them but that wasn't the way I was raised, for I was taught to share but that "my stuff" attitude crept in. It wasn't until I realized that nothing is "mine" - everything I may have is a gift - a blessing if you will, from God - so really I am only sharing the things of God with others.. then one day I read today's scripture and came to understand that "my stuff" is really His Stuff to be shared .. so I ask, need to borrow anything, it's okay with me, how about you and "your stuff", are you sharing it?

Peace,
Tom

JOHN 14:6

Jesus said to him,
"I am the way, and the truth, and the life;
no one comes to the Father but through Me.

We arrived on the second alarm call of a large warehouse fully involved in fire, we were told to go to the building next door to see if the fire had gotten that far.. I followed my officer as we entered the building and made our way to the second floor, the smoke had already become very dense making the way very difficult.. as we searched for the fire, we became disorientated.. we began searching for a way out when I heard my officer yell - over here, the way out is over here.. as I think back to that night, I am reminded of today's scripture.. there is only one Way, one Truth and one Life.. sometimes life can be like navigating through a darkened building filled with smoke, not sure which way to go, but Jesus will always lead us home, that's if we follow..

Peace,
Tom

JOHN 1:1

In the beginning was the Word,
and the Word was with God,
and the Word was God.

I sat and thought the other day where my love for Christ and the Bible started.. you would have thought that it was because my parents brought me to church, or saying grace before meals or even the evening prayers as we knelt by my bed - now I am sure those all were part of it, but the one thing that sticks out in my mind most was the fishing trips.. I know, seems kind of weird that fishing trips would have brought me to a love of Christ.. You see, my dad would play tapes in the car ride to the fishing spots.. between Johnny Cash songs, dad would throw in tapes from Katherine Kulman.. she was a woman preacher who shared some great messages from the Bible.. listening to those gave me a great beginning.. like today's verse shares, in the beginning was the Word.. we should start everyday with the Word.. some great breakfast food for the spiritual day ahead.. so the question is, how are you beginning your day?

Peace,
Tom

PROVERBS 19:17

One who is gracious to a poor man lends to the Lord,
and He will repay him for his good deed.

As I sat in my suit, waiting to speak to the pastors at a recent men's conference, I noticed him.. most would have walk past him because of the dirty clothing he wore, or the "odor" that came from his direction but I thought to myself what would Jesus do.. so I went over and asked him his name, where he came from and we engaged in a friendly conversation.. as the conference began, we both parted ways to sit and listen to the speakers.. it was during the lunch break that today's scripture came true for me, you see at lunch, I happened to spill some of my sandwich on my suit and who was there to give me a napkin and help clean me up.. yup the friend I had made earlier.. you never know when scriptures will come alive.. but then again the Bible is the living breathing Word of God.. don't pass up an opportunity to live it out!

Peace,
Tom

1 TIMOTHY 2:8

Therefore I want the men in every place to pray,
lifting up holy hands, without wrath and dissension.

During my time on the fire dept, I have worked on crews where everything went well at a fire. I have also worked on crews where when we arrived on the fire scene, things went wrong, terribly wrong. The major difference between the crews that worked well together and those that did not was dissension... even as we worked around the fire house, the crews that gelled, got things done, where the crews that did not gel, things went bad. When we work together as a team, whether at work, or at home with our families, and even at our places of worship, when we have unity, we have progress in the right direction... that goes for our prayer as well...when we are all on the same page praying for something, good things happen...when there is wrath or dissension among people, things just don't seem to go as well...maybe if we all tried to get along with each other, our prayers may have different results...just a thought... and the person causing the difficulty may just be ourselves...a good place to start!..

Peace,
Tom

PROVERBS 22:6

Train up a child in the way he should go,
Even when he is old he will not depart from it.

Not all of the days on the fire dept. are spent putting out fires, sometimes it was preventing them.. some of my favorite memories on the fire dept. were the times when the school children would enjoy a field trip to the fire house.. most guys didn't like doing the visits but I loved them.. it was an opportunity to share with the children about the dangers of playing with fire, about not being afraid of the fire fighters who would come to their homes if ever on fire or needed help. At the end of one of those days, a young boy came up and gave me a big hug.. I asked him what that hug was for.. he simply said "to keep you safe".. training up children in the way they should go, like today's verse shares, can have some great results, that's if we take the time to share with them.. when was the last time you spent some quality time with a child.. even if it's wasn't your own.. trust me, they will remember it and you will too!

Peace,
Tom

GALATIANS 6:2

Bear one another's burdens,
and thereby fulfill the law of Christ.

It didn't require any heavy lifting.. sometimes we think that helping someone out will take either muscle or some financial giving out of our part but this one particular day, it cost me neither.. today's verse shares about bearing one another's burdens and the only thing it cost me was time.. he was looking for someone just to listen, to hear his story, to feel his pain.. as we sat, he did the talking and I listened, sounds pretty funny for a partially deaf guy but just letting him share his story to someone, anyone seemed to bring him comfort.. he wasn't looking for me to fix it, or really to do anything but listen.. by the end of our time together, he said he felt better for sharing.. I felt the same too, that in one small way, for a short time, I could bear his burdens.. when was the last time you carried a friend for a little while.. why not do it today!

Peace,
Tom

1 PETER 5:8

Be of sober spirit, be on the alert.
Your adversary, the devil,
prowls around like a roaring lion,
seeking someone to devour.

As we loaded the hose after putting out the fire, the rookie came up to me and raised his hand to give me a high five. The fire had devoured the home of a family of four; all their earthly belongings had gone up in smoke. The Red Cross was called to find them some place to stay for a while until they got things straighten out as to where they were going to live now. As the rookie raised his hand to me, I took him aside and said, let's not go around giving high fives for what we just did, we put the fire out but the family lost so much.. we need to be of sober spirit when it comes to things like this and keep perspective about what has really taken place.. in life, we must be alert to the things that can devour our perspective.. like the fire that devours a home and the belongings inside, Satan wants nothing more that to devour us.. so let's be on alert!

Peace,
Tom

1 THESSALONIANS 5:11

*Therefore encourage one another
and build up one another,
just as you also are doing.*

It was just a simple dinner but it was more about the fellowship than the food.. sometimes getting together with friends can make things better - my wife and I got together with some old friends for a bite to eat, we shared stories, laughs, some of our struggles and pain, but when all was said and done, we came away encouraged - today's verse shares that exact point! When we gather with friends to encourage and spend time together, we come away a little bit stronger, a little bit happier, and ready to face the struggles of life.. so why not make the call to an old friend and do some encouraging today, you will come away blessed, I promise!

Peace,
Tom

PHILIPPIANS 3:13

*Brethren,
I do not regard myself as having laid hold of it yet;
but one thing I do: forgetting what lies behind
and reaching forward to what lies ahead,*

It can be debilitating.. thinking of the times of pain that we all have endured. Whether the pain was caused by our own actions or actions of others, it can keep us from moving forward.. or we can grab hold of today's verse and begin to reach forward to what lies ahead. I have been through some pretty rough patches of life, maybe you have too.. mine were mostly caused by my anger problems but I remained faithful to what lies ahead.. instead of what laid behind.. though never forgotten, those times can be forgiven, so let's forgive and move forward.. there is a whole world waiting for you.. and God wants to be the most important part of your future.. so why not let Him guide us forward today!

Peace,
Tom

PSALM 32:8

*I will instruct you and teach you
in the way which you should go;
I will counsel you with My eye upon you.*

The weeks leading up to my carpel tunnel surgery found me a little anxious about what to expect after surgery…I didn't want to lose any mobility or strength in my hands due to the operation…I had asked many people about their experience and even checked on line about what to expect but I found the best comfort in the words of my doctor…do what I tell you to do and you'll be fine! Sometimes in life we may find ourselves a little anxious or even nervous about the life situations we encounter…wondering what the best course of action to take is…sometimes it can get so bad that we find ourselves almost to the point of letting it consume us…take comfort for today's verse gives us some great advice about who to turn to during those moments when we just aren't sure…when we wonder which way to go…and like my doctor said, if we follow His advice, we'll be just fine…so the question is, are we following His Advice…or even seeking it for that matter…

Peace,
Tom

EPHESIANS 4:22-24

*[22] that, in reference to your former manner of life,
you lay aside the old self, which is being corrupted
in accordance with the lusts of deceit,
[23] and that you be renewed in the spirit of your mind,
[24] and put on the new self, which in the likeness of God
has been created in righteousness and holiness of the truth.*

I had to make a decision.. was I in it for the money or for helping people.. when I decided to start my handyman business, I had to make some decisions of what kind of business I was going to run.. was it going to be all about how much money I could make or was it going to be about helping people.. the business started out because some "mature" people needed some help around their homes.. little things, like fixing this and doing that, and then it led to bigger jobs.. the whole reason the business began was to use my talents and gifts to help people.. so why would I want to change the way it began.. it's not about having deceitful desires, like today's verse shares, it's about being created in the likeness of God.. so facing a new beginning, make sure you have a renewed spirit in your mind of what He wants, not what the world says you should have..

Peace,
Tom

Made in the USA
Middletown, DE
30 August 2020